Signatures

HOLISTIC READING ASSESSMENT

TEACHER'S EDITION

GRADE

1

Senior Author

Roger C. Farr

HARCOURT
BRACE

ISBN 0-15-307779-4

1 2 3 4 5 6 7 8 9 10   022   99 98 97 96

TABLE OF CONTENTS

ASSESSMENT AND EVALUATION IN *SIGNATURES*

by Roger C. Farr

Assessment gets much attention these days. There is no lessening of the plea for accountability. A wide range of informal and formal assessments is being touted as the solution to classroom assessment. We hear a great deal about authentic assessments, portfolio assessments, performance assessments, kid-watching, running-records, anecdotal records, and holistic assessments, to name just some of the terms being used.

Every good assessment program should be more than a willy-nilly collection of tests, observations, and checklists. An assessment program should be integral to instruction. The Harcourt Brace assessments have been carefully designed to provide teachers and schools with the information they need at the time they need that information. The Harcourt Brace assessments provide a comprehensive picture of students' achievements as they progress through the program. That picture will provide the basis for school and classroom planning.

Thinking about assessment as an attempt to get a picture of what students are learning and are able to do provides a useful analogy. When a teacher or school gets a valid look at where students are and what they are able to do, they can plan what they need to do to complete the picture. If we think of assessment as a picture on an easel, we can consider the three main components of assessment that hold up that easel. These three legs delineate the three main purposes for assessment: 1) finding out what students know; 2) determining if they can apply what they know; and 3) learning about students' abilities to self-assess.

The first leg of the assessment easel is to find out what students know. There is no question that students need to know skills and strategies, to comprehend literal meanings, and to recognize letters and words. There is a place for knowing, and good assessment provides information about what students know. Short-answer and multiple-choice assessments can provide useful information about what students know. Teacher observation, student work samples, and teacher/student discussions are also valuable sources of information about what students know.

The second leg of assessment is to determine if students can apply what they know. Knowing by itself is not enough. Students have to apply what they know. Finding out if students can apply what they know is the second leg of the assessment easel. Good readers and writers solve problems, read between the lines, and create their own stories and interpretations of what they read. Performance assessments, holistic writing activities, and

Harcourt Brace School Publishers • Holistic Reading Assessment

classroom portfolios are crucial if teachers are to find out whether students can go beyond just knowing to applying. Good performance assessments and activities should be integrated with instruction and should provide realistic activities that engage a student's mind.

The third leg of assessment is to engage students in self-assessment. If students are to continue to learn, they must be able to self-assess. They have to review their ideas, their projects, and their writing and learn how to improve what they are doing. Those who are successful in the world are those who learn how to figure out a way to do it better. This third leg of assessment combines instruction and assessment. As you help students to self-assess, they begin to self-assess. You watch them progress as self-assessors. They apply what they learn to become more effective readers and writers. Portfolio conferences, teacher/student discussions of work samples, and similar activities are all part of helping students become more effective self-assessors.

These three legs of the assessment easel were the basis for planning the Harcourt Brace assessments. You may want to examine the assessments in the Harcourt Brace program with this outline in mind. *Which of the assessments help to determine what students know? Which of the assessments focus on the application of what students know? Which of the assessments help students to become more effective self-assessors?*

Listed below is a brief overview of the assessment tools available in *Signatures.*

Integrated Performance Assessment
Six Integrated Performance Assessments correlated to themes in the student anthologies are available at each level of the program. These reading-writing tasks give students opportunities to construct personal interpretations of authentic literature and to apply their writing skills in meaningful situations. Holistic scoring of student responses gives a global picture of reading and writing performance.

Holistic Reading Assessment
Six Holistic Reading Assessments correlated to themes in the student anthologies are also available at each level of the program. Based on authentic reading selections, these assessments use a combination of multiple-choice and open-ended items to evaluate reading comprehension. A single, holistic score provides a snapshot of how students are progressing in the program.

Skills Assessment
Six Skills Assessments are available at each level of the program. They assess the major reading skills of decoding, vocabulary, comprehension, literary appreciation, and study skills, and the major grammar skills taught in *Signatures.* At grades 1 and 2, a separate

Phonemic Awareness Interview provides an informal assessment of a child's level of phonemic awareness to help the teacher plan for the development of literacy activities. The Skills Assessments may be used to diagnose students who are exhibiting difficulties or to evaluate progress in skills instruction.

Placement and Individual Inventory Teacher's Guide

This resource contains three assessment components. The Placement Test is a multiple-choice test that uses authentic reading selections similar to those the student will encounter in the program. It can be used individually or in large groups to estimate the appropriate level at which to place students.

The Emergent Literacy Assessment is an informal procedure for gathering information about a young child's past literacy experiences and for determining the appropriate placement in the program.

The Individual Diagnostic Inventory provides an additional tool for assessing a student's oral reading, comprehension, and writing. It may be used to diagnose strengths and weaknesses, to monitor progress in oral reading, and to evaluate instruction.

Portfolio Assessment Teacher's Guide

This assessment resource offers suggestions for initiating, maintaining, and evaluating student collections of reading and writing activities; guidelines and suggestions for conducting portfolio conferences; and ideas for sharing portfolios with parents, other teachers, and administrators. Also included in this Teacher's Guide are numerous suggestions and strategies for engaging students in self-assessment.

HOLISTIC READING ASSESSMENT

Description of the Assessments

The *Holistic Reading Assessments* are criterion-referenced assessments. The primary purpose of this assessment component is to monitor a child's progress as he or she proceeds through the *Signatures* program. The assessments evaluate reading comprehension in a global and holistic manner and help determine if a child can read adequately at the level being taught in *Signatures*.

At Grade 1, six *Holistic Reading Assessments* are available—one for each instructional book used at this grade level. Each assessment consists of two reading selections. All of the selections have been taken from children's literature and reflect the trend to use authentic reading passages to assess comprehension. The passages used on the assessments have been selected to reflect the same themes used in the instructional program. Each reading passage is preceded by a "purpose for reading" that helps children to focus on the passage.

Both multiple-choice and open-ended items are used on each assessment to ensure a more comprehensive assessment of comprehension. Following each reading passage are three multiple-choice reading comprehension questions and one open-ended question. Children are asked to respond to the open-ended items by drawing, labeling, or writing. Guidelines are provided for scoring the responses to the open-ended items. The questions have been written to assess a variety of types of comprehension.

Variations in Format and Administration

The format and the procedures for administering the *Holistic Reading Assessments* vary from book to book to reflect the developmental changes children undergo during Grade 1. Every attempt has been made to keep the assessments child-friendly and nonthreatening to emergent readers. The following table summarizes key differences in format and administration for the six *Holistic Reading Assessments* at Grade 1.

Harcourt Brace School Publishers • Holistic Reading Assessment

SUMMARY OF ASSESSMENT FORMATS AND METHODS OF ADMINISTRATION

Book	Multiple-Choice Items	Open-Ended Items	Administration
K/1	Items consist only of art; no text is used	Children draw; labeling and writing are suggested but optional	Teacher leads two shared readings; class does a choral reading; teacher reads questions and options aloud
1	Items consist only of art; no text is used	Children draw; labeling and writing are suggested but optional	Teacher leads a shared reading; teacher reads questions and options aloud
2	Items consist of art in combination with words and short phrases	Children draw; labeling and writing are encouraged	Teacher leads a shared reading; teacher reads questions and options aloud
3	Items consist of art in combination with words and short phrases	Children draw; labeling and writing are encouraged	Teacher leads a shared reading; teacher reads questions and options aloud
4	Items consist of text in combination with words and short phrases	Children draw; labeling and writing are encouraged	Children read passages and questions independently
5	Items consist only of text; no art is used	Children draw; labeling and writing are encouraged	Children read passages and questions independently

GENERAL ASSESSMENT CONSIDERATIONS

Before Getting Started

The following suggestions will help to provide a valid and reliable assessment.

1. Be thoroughly familiar with the *Holistic Reading Assessment* before beginning to administer the assessment. One way to become familiar with any assessment is to administer the assessment to yourself to alert you to any procedural difficulties your children may encounter.

2. Attempt to seat the children so that you can easily observe them. This will help you not only determine if children are on the correct page when the assessments are started but also see that they mark answers to the items appropriately.

3. Be sure that each child has a pencil to mark responses and has written his or her name on the front of the assessment booklet.

4. Have on hand a demonstration copy of a student booklet as well as the directions for administering the assessment found in this manual. The general directions to the examiner are printed in regular type. The specific directions to be read aloud to the children are printed in *italic* type.

Scheduling the Assessment

It is suggested that each assessment be administered in one sitting. The *Holistic Reading Assessment* is not a timed assessment. Most children will be able to complete the two reading passages and accompanying questions in approximately thirty to forty-five minutes.

SPECIFIC ASSESSMENT DIRECTIONS

Directions for *Rhythm and Rhyme/ Book K/1*

Write each child's name on an assessment booklet before distributing the booklets; or, if you prefer, distribute the booklets and have children write in their names. When administering the assessment, read the directions as they are written, using a natural tone and manner. If necessary, rephrase the directions in your own words to help children better understand what is required of them. Do not, however, give help on specific assessment questions. Pace directions so that all children have time to answer. Directions that should be read to children are printed in *italic* type. Directions that are for your information only (not to be read to children) are printed in regular type.

Prior to administering the assessment, read the following general directions to children.

Say: *Today we will be doing something special. We are going to do some reading together. Then you will answer questions about what we have read in this booklet. I will help you by reading the stories and the questions out loud as you follow along silently. You will show me your answer by filling in a circle under a picture in the booklet. When you answer the questions about what we have read together, it will help me know how well you understood the story. Some of the questions will be easy for you, and some may seem harder. Do the best you can on each one. Now open your booklet to page 1.*

Draw a big numeral 1 on the board. Walk around and make sure each child is on page 1.

Say: *Look at the top of the page. There is a short story called "A Good Day at School." Put your finger beside the story at the top of page 1 so I will know that you are in the right place.*

Hold up a copy of the booklet and show where the short sample story is found. Walk around and make sure all children have found the sample story.

Say: *First let me read you a question about the story.*

Read the purpose question under the title out loud.

Say: *"Why was this a special day?" Think about this question as we read the story together. Listen carefully and follow along silently while I read the story out loud.*

Read the following out loud:

A Good Day at School

Timmy rode on the bus to school.
It was a special day!
A firefighter brought a fire truck
for the children to see.
The firefighter talked to the class
about fire safety.

Harcourt Brace School Publishers • Holistic Reading Assessment

Say: *Now find question number 1 under the story. Put your finger on question number 1 and look at the three pictures beside the number 1.*

Hold up a copy of the assessment booklet to show where question number 1 is located. Check to see that all children have found the place under the story where the first question appears.

Say: *Listen carefully as I read you question number 1. "How did Timmy get to school?" Which picture shows how Timmy got to school? Did he walk with his mother? Did he go in a car? Did he ride the bus?*

Call on a volunteer to answer the question.

Say: *That's right. The story said that Timmy rode on the bus. That is why the circle has been filled in under the picture that shows Timmy getting on a bus.*

Now I am going to tell you how to mark your answers to questions. For each question, you will look at all the pictures, choose the best answer, and then you will use your pencil to fill in the circle under the picture you chose. If you change your mind, erase your mark completely. Then you can fill in the circle under the picture that you do want.

Demonstrate on the board how to mark the correct answer.

Say: *Now you will answer a question by yourself. Find question number 2 on this page. Put your finger on question number 2 and look at the three pictures beside the number 2.*

Check to see that all children have found the second question under the story.

Say: *Listen carefully as I read you question number 2. "Which picture shows who came to talk to Timmy's class?" Was it a firefighter? Was it a police officer? Was it a doctor?*

Use your pencil to fill in the circle under the picture that shows who came to talk to Timmy's class. Remember, if you change your mind, erase your answer carefully and fill in the circle under the answer you do want.

Say: *Which answer did you mark?*

Pause for replies.

Say: *Yes, that's right. A firefighter came to talk to Timmy's class. You should have filled in the circle under the picture of the firefighter. If you did not mark the right answer, erase your mark completely and fill in the circle under the firefighter.*

Raise your hand if you have a question about how to mark your answers to the questions.

Answer any questions children may have. Check to make sure all children have marked the sample correctly. Help any children who are having difficulty.

Say: *Now we will read some longer stories, and you will answer questions about what we read. Turn to the next page in your booklet, page 2.*

Be sure all children are on the right page.

Say: *I am going to read the story that begins on page 2. The story is called "Maxie and the Taxi." I will read the whole story first while you follow along silently. Then I will read the story again while you follow along silently. The third time we will all read the story out loud together. First let me read you a question about the story.*

Read the purpose question aloud.

Say: *"What does Maxie do?"*

Think about this question as we read the story together. Listen carefully and follow along silently while I read the whole story.

Harcourt Brace School Publishers • Holistic Reading Assessment

Read "Maxie and the Taxi" aloud, beginning on page 2 and continuing on page 3. Emphasize the rhythm and rhyme of the story as you read. After you finish reading the whole story, say the following.

Say: *Now let's look back on page 2.*

Check to see that all children are on page 2.

Say: *Listen carefully and follow along while I read the story again.*

Read "Maxie and the Taxi" out loud for the second time. When you finish, say the following.

Say: *Now let's read the story out loud as a class. Look on page 2 and find the beginning of the story.*

Check to see that all children are on page 2 at the beginning of the story.

Say: *Let's read together.*

Lead a choral reading of the story. After reading the story as a group say the following.

Say: *Turn to page 4. Look at the top of page 4 and find question number 1. Put your finger on question number 1 and look at the three pictures beside the number 1. Listen carefully as I read you question number 1. Which picture shows what Maxie likes to drive? Does he like to drive a bus? Does he like to drive a taxi? Does he like to drive a boat? Fill in the circle under the picture that shows what Maxie likes to drive in the story.*

Pause and wait for all children to mark their answers.

Say: *Now find question number 2 on this page. Put your finger on question number 2 and look at the three pictures beside the number 2. Which picture shows where Maxie took*

the people? Did he take them to a farm? Did he take them to the city? Did he take them to school? Fill in the circle under the picture that shows where Maxie took the people.

Pause and wait for all children to mark their answers.

Say: *Now find question number 3 on this page. Put your finger on question number 3 and look at the three pictures beside the number 3. Which picture shows what the people saw? Did they see a cow? Did they see a dog? Did they see some sheep? Fill in the circle under the picture that shows what the people saw.*

Pause and wait for all children to mark their answers.

Say: *Now turn to page 5 in your booklet. Find question number 4 on this page. I want you to draw a picture in this box. Listen carefully and follow along as I read the question. "What did Maxie and the people do at the end of the story?" Think about what happened at the end of the story and then draw a picture that shows what happened. When you have finished drawing, try to write some words under your picture that tell about what you drew. Do not worry about spelling or handwriting. If you want to use a word that you do not know how to spell, just try to spell the word as best you can.*

Encourage children to label their drawings. Some children may be capable of writing only a single word to identify what they've drawn; however, if others are capable of writing phrases or complete sentences, encourage them to do so.

Say: *Does everyone understand what you are to do?*

Provide help for any child who has difficulty. Allow sufficient time for children to complete the open-ended activity before beginning the next passage.

Harcourt Brace School Publishers • Holistic Reading Assessment

Say: *Now turn to page 6 in your booklet.*

If necessary, draw a big number 6 on the board. Check to make sure all children have found the correct page.

Say: *We are going to read another story together. The name of this story is "Walking Through the Forest." We will read this story the same way. First I will read it out loud two times, and then we will read it together. When we have finished reading the story, you will answer some questions about the story. First let me read you a question about the story.*

Read the purpose question under the title out loud.

Say: *"What did the children see as they walked through the forest?" Think about this question as we read the story together. Listen carefully and follow along silently while I read the story out loud.*

Read "Walking Through the Forest" aloud, beginning on page 6 and continuing on page 7. Again, emphasize the rhythm and rhyme of the story as you read. After you finish reading the whole story, say the following.

Say: *Now let's look back on page 6.*

Check to see that all children are on page 6.

Say: *Listen carefully and follow along while I read the story again.*

Read "Walking Through the Forest" out loud for the second time. When you finish, say the following.

Say: *Now let's read the story out loud as a class. Look on page 6 and find the beginning of the story.*

Check to see that all children are on page 6 at the beginning of the story.

Say: *Let's read together.*

Lead a choral reading of the story. After reading the story as a group, say the following.

Say: *Now turn to page 8. Look at the top of page 8 and find question number 5. Put your finger on question number 5 and look at the three pictures beside the number 5. Listen carefully as I read the question for number 5. Which picture shows where the children went walking in the story? Did they go walking in a forest? Did they go walking by a lake? Did they go walking on a street? Fill in the circle under the picture that shows where the children went walking.*

Pause and wait for all children to mark their answers.

Say: *Now find question number 6 on this page. Put your finger on question number 6 and look at the three pictures beside the number 6. Which picture shows the animal that says, "Caw, caw"? Did the fox say "Caw, caw"? Did the squirrel say, "Caw, caw"? Did the crow say "Caw, caw"? Fill in the circle under the picture that shows the animal that said, "Caw, caw."*

Pause and wait for all children to mark their answers.

Say: *Now find question number 7. Put your finger on question number 7 and look at the three pictures beside the number 7. "Which picture shows the animal the children did not want to follow them?" Did they not want the owl to follow them? Did they not want the skunk to follow them? Did they not want the fox to follow them? Fill in the circle under the picture that shows the animal the children did not want to follow them.*

Pause and wait for all children to mark their answers.

Harcourt Brace School Publishers • Holistic Reading Assessment

Say: *Now turn to page 9. Find question 8 on this page. I want you to draw a picture in this box. Listen carefully and follow along as I read the question. When the children went walking in the woods, they saw lots of animals. "What was one of the animals the children wanted to follow them?" Think about all the animals in the story and then draw a picture that shows one of the animals the children wanted to have follow them. When you have finished drawing, try to write some words under your picture that tell about what you drew. Do not worry about spelling or handwriting. If you want to use a word that you do not know how to spell, just try to spell the word as best you can.*

Encourage children to label their drawings. Some children may be capable of writing only a single word to identify what they've drawn; however, if others are capable of writing phrases or complete sentences, encourage them to do so.

Say: *Does everyone understand what you are to do?*

Provide help for any child who has difficulty.

Allow sufficient time for children to complete the open-ended activity. Tell children this is the end of the testing and collect the assessment booklets.

Optional Responding to Reading Activity

If you wish to have children complete the Optional Responding to Reading Activity, follow the guidelines provided here and use your own words to make clear to children what they are to do. Have children turn to the "Just for Fun" page at the end of the second story. Read aloud the instructions on that page as children follow along silently. Explain that this is a drawing/writing activity that is just for fun and that there are no right or wrong answers for this activity. Point out that children may all have different answers, depending on what part of the stories they liked best. Answer any questions the children may have about the activity, emphasizing that this is only for pleasure and will not be scored. Allow as much time as you wish for children to complete the optional activity.

Directions for *Picture Perfect*/Book 1

Write each child's name on an assessment booklet before distributing the booklets; or, if you prefer, distribute the booklets and have children write in their names. When administering the assessment, read the directions as they are written, using a natural tone and manner. If necessary, rephrase the directions in your own words to help children better understand what is required of them. Do not, however, give help on specific assessment questions. Pace directions so that all children have time to answer. Directions that should be read to children are printed in *italic* type. Directions that are for your information only (not to be read to children) are printed in regular type.

Prior to administering the assessment, read the following general directions to children.

Say: *Today we will be doing something special. We are going to do some reading together. Then you will answer questions about what we have read in this booklet. I will help you by reading the stories and the questions out loud as you follow along silently. You will show me your answer by filling in a circle under a picture in the booklet. When you answer the questions about what we have read together, it will help me know how well you understood the reading. Some of the questions will be easy for you, and some may seem harder. Do the best you can on each one. Now open your booklet to page 1.*

Harcourt Brace School Publishers • Holistic Reading Assessment

Draw a big numeral 1 on the board. Walk around and make sure each child is on page 1.

Say: *Look at the top of page 1. There is a short story called "A Good Day at School." Put your finger beside the story at the top of page 1 so I will know that you are in the right place.*

Hold up a copy of the booklet and show where the short sample story is found. Walk around and make sure all children have found the sample story.

Say: *First let me read you a question about the story.*

Read the purpose question under the title out loud.

Say: *"Why was this a special day?" Think about this question as we read the story together. Listen carefully and follow along silently while I read the story out loud.*

Read the following out loud:

A Good Day at School

Timmy rode on the bus to school.
It was a special day!
A firefighter brought a fire truck
for the children to see.
The firefighter talked to the class
about fire safety.

Say: *Now find question number 1 under the story. Put your finger on question number 1 and look at the three pictures beside the number 1.*

Hold up a copy of the assessment booklet to show where question number 1 is located. Check to see that all children have found the place under the story where the first question appears.

Say: *Listen carefully as I read you question number 1. "How did Timmy get to school?" Which picture shows how Timmy got to school? Did he walk with his mother? Did he go in a car? Did he ride the bus?*

Call on a volunteer to answer the question.

Say: *That's right. The story said that Timmy rode on the bus. That is why the circle has been filled in under the picture that shows Timmy getting on a bus.*

Now I am going to tell you how to mark your answers to questions. For each question, you will look at all the pictures, choose the best answer, and then you will use your pencil to fill in the circle under the picture you chose. If you change your mind, erase your mark completely. Then you can fill in the circle under the picture that you do want.

Demonstrate on the board how to mark the correct answer.

Say: *Now you will answer a question by yourself. Find question number 2 on this page. Put your finger on question number 2 and look at the three pictures beside the number 2.*

Check to see that all children have found the second question under the story.

Say: *Listen carefully as I read you question number 2. Which picture shows who came to talk to Timmy's class? Was it a firefighter? Was it a police officer? Was it a doctor?*

Use your pencil to fill in the circle under the picture that shows who came to talk to Timmy's class. Remember, if you change your mind, erase your answer carefully and fill in the circle under the answer you do want.

Say: *Which answer did you mark?*

Pause for replies.

Say: *Yes, that's right. A firefighter came to talk to Timmy's class. You should have filled in the circle under the picture of the firefighter. If you did not mark the right answer, erase your mark completely and fill in the circle under the firefighter.*

Raise your hand if you have a question about how to mark your answers to the questions.

Answer any questions children may have. Check to make sure all children have marked the sample correctly. Help any children who are having difficulty.

Say: *Now we will read some longer stories, and you will answer questions about what we read. Turn to the next page in your booklet, page 2.*

Be sure all children are on the right page.

Say: *We are going to read the story that begins on page 2. It is called "On Mother's Day." I will read the whole story first while you follow along silently. Then I will go back to the beginning of the story and read the first part again to help you answer some questions. First let me read you a question about the story.*

Read the purpose question under the title out loud.

Say: *"What surprise did the children make?" Think about this question as we read the story together. Listen carefully and follow along silently while I read the whole story.*

Read "On Mother's Day" aloud, beginning on page 2. After reading each section, have children turn their pages and follow along. After you finish reading the whole story, say the following.

Say: *Now let's turn back to page 2.*

Check to see that all children are on page 2.

Say: *Listen carefully and follow along while I read the first part of the story again.*

Reread page 2 out loud.

Say: *Now look at the top of page 3 where you see question number 1. Put your finger on question number 1 and look at the three pictures beside the number 1. Which picture shows what the children picked in the story? Did the children pick some apples? Did the children pick some flowers? Did the children pick some corn? Fill in the circle under the picture that shows what the children picked in the story.*

Pause and wait for all children to mark their answers.

Say: Now turn to page 4 in your booklet. Listen carefully and follow along while I read the last part of the story again.

Reread page 4 out loud.

Say: *Now look at the top of page 5. Find question number 2 on this page. Put your finger on question number 2 and look at the three pictures beside the number 2. Which picture shows who received a surprise on this special day? Did Mother receive a surprise? Did the dog receive a surprise? Did the children receive a surprise? Fill in the circle under the picture that shows who received a surprise on this special day.*

Pause and wait for all children to mark their answers.

Say: *Now find question number 3 on this page. Put your finger on question number 3 and look at the three pictures beside the number 3. Which picture shows how Mother felt when she got the surprise? Was Mother angry when she got her surprise? Was Mother sad when she got her surprise? Was Mother happy when she got her surprise? Fill in the circle under the picture that shows how Mother felt when she got her surprise.*

Harcourt Brace School Publishers • Holistic Reading Assessment

Pause and wait for all children to mark their answers.

Say: *The last question at the end of this story is different. Look at page 6 in your booklet. Find question number 4 on this page. I want you to draw a picture in this box. Listen carefully and follow along as I read the question. "What gift do you think the children gave their mother?" Think about all the gifts they might want to give to their mother and then draw a picture that shows one of the gifts they might have given to their mother. When you have finished drawing, try to write some words under your picture that tell about what you drew. Do not worry about spelling or handwriting. If you want to use a word that you do not know how to spell, just try to spell the word as best you can.*

Encourage children to label their drawings. Some children may be capable of writing only a single word to identify what they've drawn; however, if others are capable of writing phrases or complete sentences, encourage them to do so.

Say: *Does everyone understand what you are to do?*

Provide help for any child who has difficulty.

Allow sufficient time for children to complete the open-ended activity before beginning the next passage.

Say: *Now turn to page 8 in your booklet.*

Check to make sure all children have found the correct page.

Say: *We are going to read another story that begins on page 8. It is called "Now What Am I?" This story is a little different because it has pictures that go along with some of the words in the story. When you see the pictures, you can use them to help you read the*

words in the story. I will read the whole story first while you follow along. Then I will come back to the beginning of the story and read the first part again to help you answer some questions. First let me read you a question about the story.

Read the purpose question under the title out loud.

Say: *"What was Jake pretending to be?" Think about this question as we read the story together. Listen carefully and follow along silently while I read the whole story.*

Read "Now What Am I?" aloud, beginning on page 8. After reading each section, have the children turn their pages and follow along. After you finish the whole passage, say the following.

Say: *Now let's turn back to page 8.*

Check to see that all children are on page 8.

Say: *Listen carefully and follow along while I read the first part of the story again.*

Reread page 8 out loud.

Say: *Now look at the top of page 9 where you see question number 5. Put your finger on question number 5 and look at the three pictures beside the number 5. Which picture shows who was guessing what Jake was pretending to be? Was Dad guessing what Jake was pretending to be? Was Mom guessing what Jake was pretending to be? Was Jake's sister guessing what Jake was pretending to be? Fill in the circle under the picture that shows who was guessing what Jake was pretending to be.*

Pause and wait for all children to mark their answers.

Say: *Now turn to page 10 in your booklet. Listen carefully and follow along while I read the next part of the story again.*

Harcourt Brace School Publishers • Holistic Reading Assessment

2nd Story

Reread page 10 out loud.

Say: *Now look at the top of page 11. Find question number 6 on this page. Put your finger on question number 6 and look at the three pictures beside the number 6. Which picture shows who Jake was at the end of the story? Was Jake pretending to be an airplane at the end of the story? Was Jake just being Jake at the end of the story? Was Jake pretending to be a tree at the end of the story? Fill in the circle under the picture that shows what Jake was pretending to be at the end of the story.*

Pause and wait for all children to mark their answers.

Say: *Find question number 7 on this page. Put your finger on question number 7 and look at the three pictures beside the number 7. Which picture shows what this story was mostly about? Was the story mostly about school? Was the story mostly about a bird? Was the story mostly about a little boy? Fill in the circle under the picture that shows what this story was mostly about.*

Pause and wait for all children to mark their answers.

Say: *The last question at the end of this story is different. Look at page 12 in your booklet. Find question number 8 on this page. I want you to draw a picture in this box. Listen carefully and follow along as I read the question. "What was Jake pretending to be in the story?" Think about all the things Jake was pretending to be and then draw a picture that shows one of the things that Jake was pretending to be. When you have finished drawing, try to write some words under your picture that tell about what you drew. Do not worry about spelling or handwriting. If you want to use a word that you do not know how to spell, just try to spell the word as best you can.*

Encourage children to label their drawings. Some children may be capable of writing only a single word to identify what they've drawn; however, if others are capable of writing phrases or complete sentences, encourage them to do so.

Say: *Does everyone understand what you are to do?*

Provide help for any child who has difficulty.

Allow sufficient time for children to complete the open-ended activity. Tell children this is the end of the testing, and collect the assessment booklets.

Optional Responding to Reading Activity

If you wish to have children complete the Optional Responding to Reading Activity, follow the guidelines provided here, and use your own words to make clear to children what they are to do. Have children turn to the "Just for Fun" page at the end of the second story. Read aloud the instructions on that page as children follow along silently. Explain that this is a drawing/writing activity that is just for fun and that there are no right or wrong answers for this activity. Point out that children may all have different answers, depending on what part of the stories they liked best. Answer any questions the children may have about the activity, emphasizing that this is only for pleasure and will not be scored. Allow as much time as you wish for children to complete the optional activity.

Directions for *Big Dreams*/Book 2

Write each child's name on an assessment booklet before distributing the booklets; or, if you prefer, distribute the booklets and have children write in their names. When administering the assessment, read the directions as they are written, using a

Harcourt Brace School Publishers • Holistic Reading Assessment

natural tone and manner. If necessary, rephrase the directions in your own words to help children better understand what is required of them. Do not, however, give help on specific assessment questions. Pace directions so that all children have time to answer. Directions that should be read to children are printed in *italic* type. Directions that are for your information only (not to be read to children) are printed in regular type.

Prior to administering the assessment, read the following general directions to children.

Say: *Today we will be doing something special. We are going to do some reading together. Then you will answer questions about what we have read in this booklet. I will help you by reading the stories and the questions out loud as you follow along silently. You will show me your answer by filling in a circle under the picture of each answer you choose. When you answer the questions about what we have read together, it will help me know how well you understood the reading. Some of the questions will be easy for you, and some may seem harder. Do the best you can on each one. Now open your booklet to page 1.*

Draw a big numeral 1 on the board. Walk around and make sure each child is on page 1.

Say: *Look at the top of page 1. There is a short story called "A Good Day at School." Put your finger beside the story at the top of page 1 so I will know that you are in the right place.*

Hold up a copy of the booklet and show where the short sample story is found. Walk around and make sure all children have found the sample story.

Say: *First let me read you a question about the story.*

Read the purpose question under the title out loud.

Say: *"Why was this a special day?" Think about this question as we read the story together. Listen carefully and follow along silently while I read the story out loud.*

Read the following out loud:

A Good Day at School

Timmy rode on the bus to school.
It was a special day!
A firefighter brought a fire truck
for the children to see.
The firefighter talked to the class
about fire safety.

Say: *Now find question number 1 under the story. Put your finger on question number 1 and look at the three pictures and words below the question.*

Hold up a copy of the assessment booklet to show where question number 1 is located. Check to see that all children have found the place under the story where the first question appears.

Say: *Follow along silently as I read question number 1 out loud. "How did Timmy get to school?" Under the first picture there is a letter A and the words "walked with Mother." Under the middle picture there is a letter B and the words "rode in a car." Under the last picture there is a letter C and the words "rode the bus." Which picture and words answer the question "How did Timmy get to school?" A? B? or C?*

Call on a volunteer to answer the question.

Say: *That's right. The story said that Timmy rode on the bus. Answer C is the best answer to question number 1.*

Harcourt Brace School Publishers • Holistic Reading Assessment

Now I am going to tell you how to mark your answers to questions. For each question, you will look at all the pictures and words, choose the best answer, and then you will use your pencil to fill in answer circle A, B, or C under the picture you chose. If you change your mind after you have filled in the answer circle, erase your mark completely. Then you can fill in the answer circle that you do want.

Demonstrate on the board how to mark the correct answer.

Say: Now use your pencil to fill in answer circle C for question number 1 because "rode the bus" is the correct answer to question 1.

Say: Now you will answer a question by yourself. Find question number 2 on this page. Put your finger on question number 2 and look at the three pictures and words below the question.

Check to see that all children have found the second question under the story.

Say: Follow along silently as I read question number 2 out loud. "Who came to talk to Timmy's class?" Which picture and words answer the question "Who came to talk to Timmy's class?" Answer A, "a firefighter"? Answer B, "a police officer"? or Answer C, "a doctor"?

Use your pencil to fill in answer circle A, B, or C that tells who came to talk to Timmy's class. Remember, if you change your mind, erase your answer carefully and fill in the answer circle you do want.

Say: Which answer did you mark?

Pause for replies.

Say: Yes, that's right. A firefighter came to talk to Timmy's class. You should have filled in answer circle A under the picture of the firefighter. If you did not fill in answer circle A, erase your mark completely and fill in answer circle A.

Raise your hand if you have a question about how to mark your answers to the questions.

Answer any questions children may have. Check to make sure all children have marked the sample correctly. Help any children who are having difficulty.

Say: Now we will read some longer stories, and you will answer questions about what we read. One of the stories is a little different because it has pictures that go along with some of the words in the story. When you see the pictures, you can use them to help you read the words in the story. Turn to the next page in your booklet, page 2. I am going to read the story that begins on page 2 out loud.

Be sure all children are on the right page. Follow the same procedures used for the sample when you administer the assessment. The steps to follow are summarized below.

1. Read the title and the purpose question aloud. Tell children to think about the purpose question as you read the story together.

2. Read the whole story aloud as children follow along silently.

3. Have children turn back to the first section of the story and the accompanying questions. Reread the first story section while the children follow along silently. Read the question(s) and the answer options out loud, pausing after each to allow children to mark their answers.

4. Reread each story section aloud to children before having them complete the accompanying questions for the section.

5. When children complete all of the multiple-choice questions for a passage, have them complete the open-

Harcourt Brace School Publishers • Holistic Reading Assessment

ended item for that passage before moving on to the next passage. Explain that the last question at the end of the story is different. Have children locate the question and the box. Tell them they will draw a picture in the box, and have them listen carefully and follow along as you read the question out loud. Tell children to think about the story and then draw a picture in the box to answer the question. Repeat the question before children begin to draw their responses. Tell children that after they have finished drawing, they should try to write some words under their pictures that tell about what they drew. Explain that they need not worry about spelling and handwriting. Tell them that if they want to use words that they do not know how to spell, they should just spell the words as best they can.

6. Encourage children to label their drawings. Some children may be capable of writing only a single word to identify what they've drawn; however, if others are capable of writing phrases or complete sentences, encourage them to do so. Provide help for any child who has difficulty. Allow sufficient time for children to complete the open-ended activity before beginning the next passage.

7. Follow the same procedures for the second story on the assessment.

8. When all children have finished working, tell them this is the end of the testing and collect the assessment booklets.

Directions for *Warm Friends*/Book 3

Write each child's name on an assessment booklet before distributing the booklets; or, if you prefer, distribute the booklets and have children write in their names. When administering the assessment, read the directions as they are written, using a natural tone and manner. If necessary, rephrase the directions in your own words to help children better understand what is required of them. Do not, however, give help on specific assessment questions. Pace directions so that all children have time to answer. Directions that should be read to children are printed in *italic* type. Directions that are for your information only (not to be read to children) are printed in regular type.

Prior to administering the assessment, read the following general directions to children.

Say: *Today we will be doing something special. We are going to do some reading together. Then you will answer questions about what we have read in this booklet. I will help you by reading the stories and the questions out loud as you follow along silently. You will show me your answer by filling in a circle under the picture of each answer you choose. When you answer the questions about what we have read together, it will help me know how well you understood the reading. Some of the questions will be easy for you, and some may seem harder. Do the best you can on each one. Now open your booklet to page 1.*

Draw a big numeral 1 on the board. Walk around and make sure each child is on page 1.

Say: *Look at the top of page 1. There is a short story called "A Good Day at School." Put your finger beside the story at the top of page 1 so I will know that you are in the right place.*

Hold up a copy of the booklet and show where the short sample story is found. Walk around and make sure all children have found the sample story.

Say: *First let me read you a question about the story.*

Read the purpose question under the title out loud.

Say: *"Why was this a special day?" Think about this question as we read the story together. Listen carefully and follow along silently while I read the story out loud.*

Read the following out loud:

A Good Day at School

> *Timmy rode on the bus to school.*
> *It was a special day!*
> *A firefighter brought a fire truck*
> *for the children to see.*
> *The firefighter talked to the class*
> *about fire safety.*

Say: *Now find question number 1 under the story. Put your finger on question number 1 and look at the three pictures and the words below the question.*

Hold up a copy of the assessment booklet to show where question number 1 is located. Check to see that all children have found the place under the story where the first question appears.

Say: *Follow along silently as I read question number 1 out loud. "How did Timmy get to school?" Under the first picture there is a letter A and the words "walked with Mother." Under the middle picture there is a letter B and the words "rode in a car." Under the last picture there is a letter C and the words "rode the bus." Which picture and words answer the question "How did Timmy get to school?" A? B? or C?*

Call on a volunteer to answer the question.

Say: *That's right. The story said that Timmy rode on the bus. Answer C is the best answer to question number 1.*

Now I am going to tell you how to mark your answers to questions. For each question, you will look at all the pictures and words, choose the best answer, and then you will use your pencil to fill in answer circle A, B, or C under the picture you chose. If you change your mind after you have filled in the answer circle, erase your mark completely. Then you can fill in the answer circle that you do want.

Demonstrate on the board how to mark the correct answer.

Say: *Now use your pencil to fill in answer circle C for question number 1 because "rode the bus" is the correct answer to question 1.*

Say: *Now you will answer a question by yourself. Find question number 2 on this page. Put your finger on question number 2 and look at the three pictures and the words below the question.*

Harcourt Brace School Publishers • Holistic Reading Assessment

Check to see that all children have found the second question under the story.

Say: *Follow along silently as I read question number 2 out loud. "Who came to talk to Timmy's class?" Which picture and words answer the question "Who came to talk to Timmy's class?" Answer A, "a firefighter"? Answer B, "a police officer"? or Answer C, a doctor"?*

Use your pencil to fill in answer circle A, B, or C that tells who came to talk to Timmy's class. Remember, if you change your mind, erase your answer carefully and fill in the answer circle you do want.

Say: *Which answer did you mark?*

Pause for replies.

Say: *Yes, that's right. A firefighter came to talk to Timmy's class. You should have filled in answer circle A under the picture of the firefighter. If you did not fill in answer circle A, erase your mark completely and fill in answer circle A.*

Raise your hand if you have a question about how to mark your answers to the questions.

Answer any questions children may have. Check to make sure all children have marked the sample correctly. Help any children who are having difficulty.

Say: *Now we will read some longer stories, and you will answer questions about what we read. One of the stories is a little different because it has pictures that go along with some of the words in the story. When you see the pictures, you can use them to help you read the words in the story. Turn to the next page in your booklet, page 2. I am going to read the story that begins on page 2 out loud.*

Be sure all children are on the right page. Follow the same procedures used for the sample when you administer the assessment. The steps to follow are summarized as follows:

1. Read the title and the purpose question aloud. Tell children to think about the purpose question as you read the story together.

2. Read the whole story aloud as children follow along silently.

3. Have children turn back to the first section of the story and the accompanying questions. Reread the first story section while the children follow along silently. Read the question(s) and the answer options out loud, pausing after each to allow children to mark their answers.

4. Reread each story section aloud to children before having them complete the accompanying questions for the section.

5. When children complete all of the multiple-choice questions for the first passage, have them complete the open-ended item for that passage before moving on to the next passage. Explain that the last question at the end of the story is different. Have children locate the question and the box. Tell them they will draw a picture in the box, and have them listen carefully and follow along as you read the question out loud. Tell children to think about the story and then draw a picture in the box to answer the question. Repeat the question before children begin to draw their responses. Tell children that after they have finished drawing, they should try to write some words under their pictures that tell about what they drew. Explain that they need not worry about spelling and handwriting. Tell them that if

Harcourt Brace School Publishers • Holistic Reading Assessment

they want to use words that they do not know how to spell, they should just spell the words as best they can.

6. Encourage children to label their drawings. Some children may be capable of writing only a single word to identify what they've drawn; however, if others are capable of writing phrases or complete sentences, encourage them to do so. Provide help for any child who has difficulty. Allow sufficient time for children to complete the open-ended activity before beginning the next passage.

7. Follow the same procedures for the second story on the assessment.

8. When all children have finished working, tell children that this is the end of the testing and collect the assessment booklets.

Directions for *Full Sails*/Book 4

Write each child's name on an assessment booklet before distributing the booklets; or, if you prefer, distribute the booklets and have children write in their names. When administering the assessment, read the directions as they are written, using a natural tone and manner. If necessary, rephrase the directions in your own words to help children better understand what is required of them. Do not, however, give help on specific assessment questions. Pace directions so that all children have time to answer. Directions that should be read to children are printed in *italic* type. Directions that are for your information only (not to be read to children) are printed in regular type.

Prior to administering the assessment, read the following general directions to children.

Say: *Today we will be doing something special. We are going to do some reading together. Then you will answer questions about what we have read in this booklet. You will read the stories and the questions to yourself silently. You will show me your answers by filling in a circle under each answer you choose. When you answer the questions about what we have read, it will help me know how well you understood the reading. Some of the questions will be easy for you, and some may seem harder. Do the best you can on each one. Now open your booklet to page 1.*

Draw a big numeral 1 on the board. Walk around and make sure each child is on page 1.

Say: *Look at the top of the page. There is a short story called "Good Friends." Put your finger beside the story at the top of page 1 so I will know that you are in the right place.*

Hold up a copy of the booklet and show where the short sample story is found. Walk around and make sure all children have found the sample story.

Harcourt Brace School Publishers • Holistic Reading Assessment

Say: *First, look at the question under the title at the top of the page, and follow along while I read it out loud.*

Read the purpose question under the title out loud.

Say: *"What do Ben and Jill want to do?" Think about this question as you read the story silently. Now read the story.*

Allow enough time for all children to read the story independently.

Say: *Now find question number 1 under the story. Put your finger on question number 1 and look at the three pictures and the words under question number 1.*

Hold up a copy of the assessment booklet to show where question number 1 is located. Check to see that all children have found the place under the story where the first question appears.

Say: *Follow along silently as I read question number 1 out loud. "Ben wants to _____ ." Answer A, "ride bikes"? Answer B, "look at TV"? or Answer C, play ball"?*

Call on a volunteer to answer the question.

Say: *That's right. In the story Ben said, "I want to play ball." Answer C is the best answer to question number 1.*

Now I am going to tell you how to mark your answers to questions. For each question, you will look at all the pictures and words, choose the best answer, and then you will use your pencil to fill in answer circle A, B, or C under the picture for the answer you chose. If you change your mind after you have filled in the answer circle, erase your mark completely. Then you can fill in the answer circle that you do want.

Demonstrate on the board how to mark the correct answer.

Say: *Now use your pencil to fill in answer circle C for question number 1 because "play ball" is the correct answer to question 1.*

Say: *Now you will answer another question by yourself. Find the number 2 on this page. Put your finger on the number 2 and read the question to yourself. Then look at the three pictures and words that are under question number 2.*

Check to see that all children have found the second question under the story.

Say: *Read question number 2 to yourself and think about the correct answer. Which picture and words answer the question?*

Use your pencil to fill in answer circle A, B, or C. Choose the best answer. Remember, if you change your mind, erase your mark carefully and fill in the answer circle you want.

Say: *Which answer did you mark?*

Pause for replies.

Say: *Yes, that's right. Father will play with Ben and Jill. You should have filled in answer circle B under the picture that shows Father. If you did not fill in answer circle B, erase your mark completely and fill in answer circle B.*

Raise your hand if you have a question about how to mark your answers to the questions.

Answer any questions children may have. Check to make sure all children have marked the sample correctly. Help any children who are having difficulty.

Say: *Now you will read two longer stories silently, and you will answer questions about what you read. One of the stories is a little different because it has pictures to go along with some of the words in the story. When you see the pictures, you can use them to help you read the words in the story. You may look back at*

Harcourt Brace School Publishers • Holistic Reading Assessment

the stories to help you choose your answers. Turn to the next page in your booklet, page 2.

Be sure all children are on the right page.

Say: *Remember to read the title and the question at the top of the page first. Think about the question at the top of the page as you read the story. After you have finished the story, you will answer four questions about what you have read.*

The last question at the end of the story is different. There is a big box at the end of the story. You are to draw a picture in this box. Turn to page 5 and find the box. (Pause for children to find page 5.)

When you get to this part, read the question above the box, then draw your picture in the box to answer the question. When you have finished drawing, try to write some words under your picture that tell about what you drew. Do not worry about spelling or handwriting. If you want to use a word that you do not know how to spell, just try to spell the word as well as you can.

Encourage children to label their drawings. Some children may be capable of writing only a single word to identify what they've drawn; however, if other children are capable of writing phrases or complete sentences, encourage them to do so.

Say: *Does everyone understand what you are to do?*

Provide help for any child who has difficulty.

When all children have finished working, tell them this is the end of the testing and collect the assessment booklets.

Optional Responding to Reading Activity

If you wish to have children complete the Optional Responding to Reading Activity, follow the guidelines provided here, and use your own words to make clear to children what they are to do. Have children turn to the "Just for Fun" page at the end of the second story. Read aloud the instructions on that page as children follow along silently. Explain that this is a drawing/writing activity that is just for fun and that there are no right or wrong answers for this activity. Point out that children may all have different answers, depending on what part of the stories they liked best. Answer any questions children may have about the activity, emphasizing that this is only for pleasure and will not be scored. Allow as much time as you wish for children to complete the optional activity.

Directions for *All Smiles*/Book 5

Write each child's name on an assessment booklet before distributing the booklets; or, if you prefer, distribute the booklets and have children write in their names. When administering the assessment, read the directions as they are written, using a natural tone and manner. If necessary, rephrase the directions in your own words to help children better understand what is required of them. Do not, however, give help on specific assessment questions. Pace directions so that all children have time to answer. Directions that should be read to children are printed in *italic* type. Directions that are for your information only (not to be read to children) are printed in regular type.

Prior to administering the assessment, read the following general directions to children.

Harcourt Brace School Publishers • Holistic Reading Assessment

Say: *Today you will be doing something special. You are going to do some reading. Then you will answer questions about what you have read in this booklet. You will read the stories and the questions to yourself silently. You will show me your answers by filling in an answer circle under each answer you choose. When you answer the questions about what you have read, it will help me know how well you understood the reading. Some of the questions will be easy for you, and some will seem harder. Do the best you can on each one. Now open your booklet to page 1.*

Draw a big numeral 1 on the board. Walk around and make sure each child is on page 1.

Say: *Look at the top of the page. There is a short story called "Good Friends." Put your finger beside the story at the top of page 1 so I will know that you are in the right place.*

Hold up a copy of the booklet and show where the short sample story is found. Walk around and make sure all children have found the sample story.

Say: *First, look at the question under the title at the top of the page, and follow along while I read it out loud.*

Read the purpose question under the title out loud.

Say: *"What do Ben and Jill want to do?" Think about this question as you read the story silently. Now read the story.*

Allow enough time for all children to read the story independently.

Say: *Now find question number 1 under the story. Put your finger on question number 1 and look at the three groups of words under question number 1.*

Hold up a copy of the assessment booklet to show where question number 1 is located. Check to see that all children have found the place under the story where the first question appears.

Say: *Follow along silently as I read question number 1 out loud. "Ben wants to _____." Answer A, "ride bikes"? Answer B, "look at TV"? or Answer C, play ball"?*

Call on a volunteer to answer the question.

Say: *That's right. In the story Ben said, "I want to play ball." Answer C is the best answer to question number 1.*

Now I am going to tell you how to mark your answers to questions. For each question, you will look at all the answers, choose the best answer, and then use your pencil to fill in answer circle A, B, or C next to the answer you chose. If you change your mind after you have filled in the answer circle, erase your mark completely. Then you can fill in the answer circle that you do want.

Demonstrate on the board how to mark the correct answer.

Say: *Now use your pencil to fill in answer circle C for question number 1 because "play ball" is the correct answer to question 1.*

Say: *Now you will answer another question by yourself. Find the number 2 on this page. Put your finger on the number 2 and read the question to yourself. Then look at the answers that are under question number 2.*

Check to see that all children have found the second question under the story.

Say: *Use your pencil to fill in answer circle A, B, or C. Choose the best answer. Remember, if you change your mind, erase your mark carefully and fill in the answer circle you do want.*

Harcourt Brace School Publishers • Holistic Reading Assessment

Say: *Which answer did you mark?*

Pause for replies.

Say: *Yes, that's right. Father will play with Ben and Jill. You should have filled in answer circle B next to the word Father. If you did not fill in answer circle B, erase your mark completely and fill in answer circle B.*

Raise your hand if you have a question about how to mark your answers to the questions.

Answer any questions children may have. Check to make sure all children have marked the sample correctly. Help any children who are having difficulty.

Say: *Now you will read two longer stories silently, and you will answer questions about what you read. You may look back at the stories to help you choose your answers. Turn to the next page in your booklet, page 2.*

Be sure all children are on the right page.

Say: *Remember to read the title and the question under the title. Think about the question at the top of the page as you read the story. After you have finished the story, you will answer four questions about what you have read.*

The last question at the end of the story is different. There is a big box at the end of the story. You are to draw a picture in this box. Turn to page 5 and find the box. (Pause for children to find page 5.)

When you get to this part, read the question above the box and then draw your picture in the box to answer the question. When you have finished drawing, try to write some words under your picture that tell about what you drew. Do not worry about spelling or handwriting. If you want to use a word that you do not know how to spell, just try to spell the word as well as you can.

Encourage children to label their drawings. Some children may be capable of writing only a single word to identify what they've drawn; however, if other children are capable of writing phrases or complete sentences, encourage them to do so.

Say: *Does everyone understand what you are to do?*

Provide help for any child who has difficulty.

When all children have finished working, tell children this is the end of the testing and collect the assessment booklets.

Optional Responding to Reading Activity

If you wish to have children complete the Optional Responding to Reading Activity, follow the guidelines provided here, and use your own words to make clear to children what they are to do. Have children turn to the "Just for Fun" page at the end of the second story. Read aloud the instructions on that page as children follow along silently. Explain that this is a drawing/writing activity that is just for fun and that there are no right or wrong answers for this activity. Point out that children may all have different answers, depending on what part of the stories they liked best. Answer any questions children may have about the activity, emphasizing that this is only for pleasure and will not be scored. Allow as much time as you wish for children to complete the optional activity.

Harcourt Brace School Publishers • Holistic Reading Assessment

SCORING AND INTERPRETING

Scoring the Multiple-Choice Items

Each of the multiple-choice assessment items is scored 1 point if the answer is correct. If the answer is incorrect or left blank, 0 points are given. Thus, the maximum number of points a child may receive on the multiple-choice items for a *Holistic Reading Assessment* is 6 points (2 passages with 3 items each).

The multiple-choice items may be scored by using either the answer keys found later in this booklet or by using the reduced facsimile pages of the student assessment booklets, which are also found later in this booklet.

Scoring the Open-Ended Items

Each of the open-ended assessment items may receive a score of 2, 1, or 0, depending on how complete and accurate the answer is. The general scoring guidelines following explain the meaning of each score.

Specific scoring guidelines for each open-ended item used at this grade level are included in the answer keys found later in this booklet.

Determining the Total Score

To arrive at a child's total score on a *Holistic Reading Assessment*, you need to combine the results of the multiple-choice items with the results of the open-ended items. The total score can range from a low of 0 points (all items incorrect) to a high of 10 points (all items correct). The total score can be easily converted for grading purposes to a 100-point scale by multiplying by 10. The following example illustrates how to determine a total score and place it on a 100-point scale

---

GENERAL SCORING GUIDELINES FOR THE OPEN-ENDED ITEMS

Score of 2:
A "Correct" Answer

The answer is correct and/or logical (or very nearly so) and is clearly based on relevant and explicit information in the passage. All parts of the question are fully answered.

Score of 1:
A "Partially Correct" Answer

The answer is partially correct and/or logical and is generally based on relevant and explicit information in the passage. Some parts of the question may not be fully answered, or the explanation may not be as explicit as a "correct" answer.

Score of 0:
An "Incorrect" Answer

The answer is incorrect for one of many reasons: it may not address the question; it may be only loosely related to the passage; it may be based only on personal opinion; or it may be off-task or irrelevant.

SAMPLE SCORING

Passage Number 1	Score
2 multiple-choice items correct	2
1 multiple-choice item incorrect	0
1 open-ended item correct	2
Passage Number 2	
3 multiple-choice items correct	3
1 open-ended item partially correct	1
Total Score	**8**
Total Score on a 100-point Scale (8 x 10)	**80**

Score	Interpretation	Teaching Suggestions
9–10	Very good reader at this level of the program	Students scoring at this level should have no difficulty moving forward in the program.
7–8	Average reader at this level of the program	Students scoring at this level may need a little extra help.
5–6	Fair reader at this level of the program	Students scoring at this level may need more help. Other samples of performance should be examined to confirm progress and pinpoint instructional needs.
Fewer than 5	Limited reader at this level of the program	Students scoring at this level will almost certainly have difficulty completing this level.

Analyzing Student Performance

The following table offers guidelines for interpreting a child's performance on the *Holistic Reading Assessment*. Remember, however, that it is important not to place too much faith in any single assessment. The *Holistic Reading Assessment* is only one sample of a child's reading. This sample should be compared to the information you have gathered from daily observations, work samples, and perhaps other assessment scores.

You may find that some children are less successful in responding to open-ended items than in answering the multiple-choice items. This may occur for a number of reasons:

- Many of the open-ended items are designed to elicit diverse responses. Some children might feel uncomfortable in approaching broad-based tasks when they are more accustomed to close-ended tasks that call for convergent answers.

- Some children may lack expertise in expressing ideas in pictorial form.

- Some children, unaccustomed to tasks of this nature, might not clearly understand what they are to do.

- It is possible for children to have good comprehension on a literal level but to experience frustration when called upon to apply and use ideas from the reading.

Alternatively, you might find that some children experience a high degree of success when responding to the open-ended items but perform less successfully when responding in the multiple-choice format. A number of explanations are possible for this:

- Some children might grasp the global meaning of a story while overlooking some of the supporting details presented.

- Children might have limited experience with taking multiple-choice tests.

- A child might view items from an unusual individual viewpoint that results in missing the obvious correct answer.

Harcourt Brace School Publishers • Holistic Reading Assessment

Although the children's picture labeling is not scored, any writing the child has provided to help identify or describe the drawing can be used to make an informal diagnosis of the child's literacy development. Both writing and spelling can be assessed in the child's picture labeling.

In evaluating a child's writing, consider the following:

- Does the child print from left to right?

- Does the child leave a space between words or groups of letters meant to represent words?

Spelling reveals a great deal about children's conceptual understanding of reading and writing. The way they print, what they print, and how they print can all provide important insights. In evaluating spelling, consider the following:

- Does the child use standard spelling?

- Does the child represent most sounds in a word, using appropriate letters to represent sounds?

- Does the child fail to discern the relationship between sounds of words to be spelled and letters used to spell the sounds?

- Does the child show no understanding of letters and/or words?

From such considerations you can infer whether a child is at a very early, transitional, or more advanced stage of literacy development. As you study your children's work, remember that your judgment is necessary in analyzing the open-ended re-sponses. After you have analyzed a few papers, the task will become easier. Teacher judgment has proved to be in-sightful, useful, and consistent in assessing reading comprehension through pictorial responses.

FIELD-TEST INFORMATION

Harcourt Brace School Publishers • Holistic Reading Assessment

The *Holistic Reading Assessments* were developed in collaboration with Dr. Roger Farr and the Center for Reading and Language Studies at Indiana University. The center was chosen because of its wide range of experience in developing language arts assessments.

The *Holistic Reading Assessment* items were written by professional test-development personnel using specifications based on the *Signatures* program. Reading selections and assessment items were field-tested during the fall of 1995. A listing of school test sites that participated in the field tests of assessment components for *Signatures* follows.

Field-Test Design

A variety of types of school districts participated in the field tests. They represented different geographic regions of the country, different socioeconomic groups, and different sizes. Participating students represented a broad range of ability levels.

All assessments were administered by regular classroom teachers and returned to Indiana University for scoring and analysis. Standardized directions were provided for each teacher. Suggested test sittings and approximate testing times were provided; however, teachers were encouraged to allow sufficient time for all children to complete the assessments.

Although each reading selection and set of comprehension questions was targeted for a particular grade level, the passages and items were tried out at more than one grade level during the field tests to gain a better estimate of item difficulty for children at various grade levels.

The item analysis data included the number and percent of children choosing each response option or omitting the item. Point-biserial item discrimination indices were also calculated for each item by grade level. These item-level statistics formed the primary sets of data used to select the final passages and items and to make appropriate item revisions.

Each participating teacher also completed a questionnaire indicating the appropriateness of the passages and items, the interest level of the materials, and the clarity of the directions.

Based on the field-test data, the final *Holistic Reading Assessments* were built by the publisher.

Field-Test Sites

Beaumont Independent School District
Beaumont, Texas

Broward County School District
Pembroke Pines, Florida

Diocese of Corpus Christi
Corpus Christi, Texas

Emery County School District
Huntington, Utah

Grantsburg School District
Grantsburg, Wisconsin

Grapevine-Colleyville Independent
    School District
Grapevine, Texas

Haddon Heights School District
Haddon Heights, New Jersey

Marion Community Unit School District #2
Marion, Illinois

Merchantville School District
Merchantville, New Jersey

Monroe County Community School
Corporation
Bloomington, Indiana

Pennsauken Public Schools
Pennsauken, New Jersey

Pine Hill Public Schools
Pine Hill, New Jersey

Rockwood School District
Rockwood, Missouri

School District of Palm Beach County
West Palm Beach, Florida

Williamsville Public Schools
Williamsville, New York

Harcourt Brace School Publishers • Holistic Reading Assessment

Reduced and Annotated Pupil Facsimile Pages

Rhythym and Rhyme/Book K/1

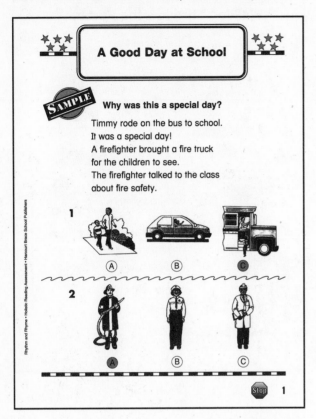

A Good Day at School

SAMPLE

Why was this a special day?

Timmy rode on the bus to school.
It was a special day!
A firefighter brought a fire truck
for the children to see.
The firefighter talked to the class
about fire safety.

1   Ⓐ   Ⓑ   Ⓒ

2   Ⓐ   Ⓑ   Ⓒ

Stop   1

Maxie and the Taxi

by Dennis Lee • Art by Toni Goffe

What does Maxie do?

Maxie drove a taxi   With a *beep! beep! beep!*

And he picked up all the people
In a heap, heap, heap.

2   Go on

He took them to the farm

To see the sheep, sheep, sheep—

Then, Maxie and the taxi
Went to sleep, sleep, sleep.

Go on   3

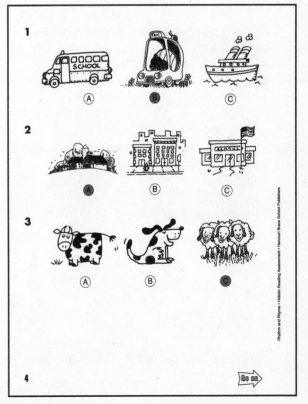

1   Ⓐ   Ⓑ   Ⓒ

2   Ⓐ   Ⓑ   Ⓒ

3   Ⓐ   Ⓑ   Ⓒ

4   Go on

T29

4 What did Maxie and the people do at the end of the story?

(Stop) **5**

Walking Through the Forest

An Action Rhyme
by Shelee C. O'Dell • Art by Joan Holub

What did the children see as they walked through the forest?

Walking through
the forest,

What do I see?

A squirrel—flip, flap!

Come and follow me.

Walking through the forest,

What do I see?

A crow—caw, caw!

Come and follow me.

6

(Go on)

Walking through the forest,

What do I see?

An owl—hoot, hoot!

Come and follow me.

Walking through the forest,

What do I see?

A fox—hehh, hehh, hehh!

Come and follow me.

Walking through the forest,

What do I smell?

A skunk—PEW!

Don't you follow me!

7 (Go on)

5

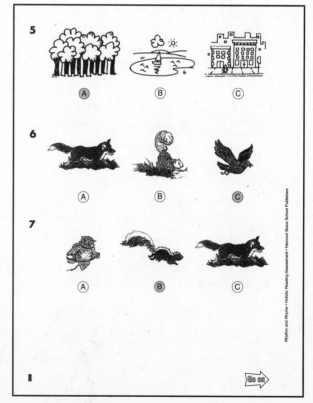

(A)   (B)   (C)

6

(A)   (B)   (C)

7

(A)   (B)   (C)

8 (Go on)

8 What was one of the animals the children wanted to follow them?

Just for Fun!

Think about the stories you just read. Then draw your favorite part of one of the stories. If you want, you may write to tell about your drawing.

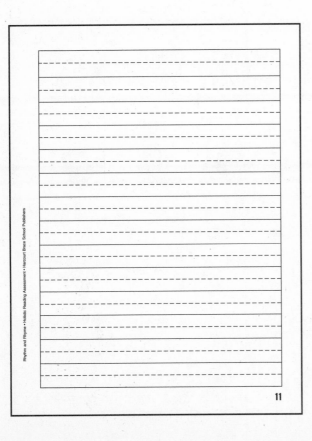

A Good Day at School

SAMPLE

Why was this a special day?

Timmy rode on the bus to school.
It was a special day!
A firefighter brought a fire truck
for the children to see.
The firefighter talked to the class
about fire safety.

1
Ⓐ   Ⓑ   Ⓒ

2
Ⓐ   Ⓑ   Ⓒ

On Mother's Day

by Aileen Fisher   Art by Kathleen Howell

What surprise did the children make?

On Mother's Day we got up first
so full of plans we almost burst.

We started breakfast right away
as our surprise for Mother's Day.

We picked some flowers, then hurried back
to make the coffee—rather black.

2   Go on ➡

1

Ⓐ   Ⓑ   Ⓒ

Go on ➡ 3

We wrapped our gifts and wrote a card
and boiled the eggs—a little hard.

And then we sang a serenade,
which burned the toast, I am afraid.

But Mother said, amidst our cheers,
"Oh, what a big surprise, my dears,
I've not had such a treat in years."
And she was smiling to her ears!

4   Go on ➡

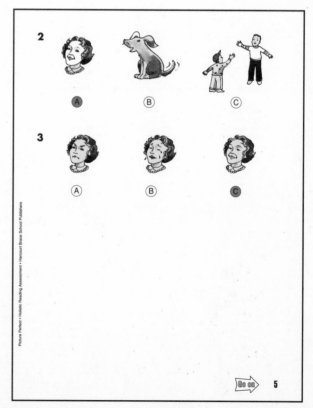

2

Ⓐ   Ⓑ   Ⓒ

3

Ⓐ   Ⓑ   Ⓒ

Go on ➡ 5

4 What gift do you think the children gave their mother?

```
2 - gifts

1 - children/mom
    no gifts

0 - 0 gifts
    0 mom
    0 children
```

6

Stop

Now What Am I?
by Diane Burns
Illustrated by Meryl Henderson

What was Jake pretending to be?

"Look,  Dad," said Jake. "Can you guess what I am?" Jake flapped his arms and said, "Jay, jay!"

"You are a blue jay, Dad guessed.

"Yes," Jake said. "Can you guess this?" He held his arms up high. He wiggled his fingers. He whispered, "Rustle, rustle, rustle."

"Are you a tree?" guessed Dad.

"Yes," said Jake.

8

Go on

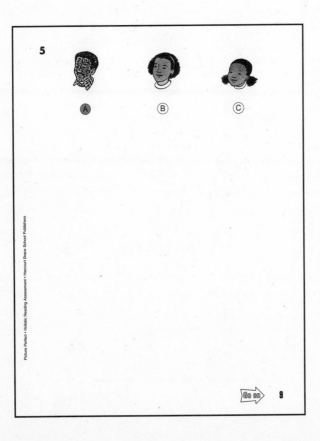

5

Ⓐ   Ⓑ   Ⓒ

Go on   9

He stuck his arms out sideways. "Now what am I? Zoom, zoom!"

"An airplane?" guessed Dad.

"Yes. Now I can do something else with my arms," Jake said. He gave Dad a big hug.

"You must be my Jake again," said Dad.

"Right!" said Jake.

"I am glad," said Dad.

10

Go on

T33

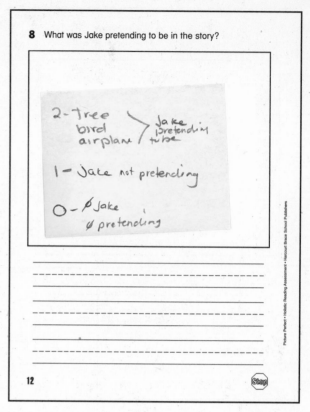

8 What was Jake pretending to be in the story?

[Handwritten notes:]
2 - Tree
    bird   ⟩ Jake pretending
    airplane ⟩ to be
1 - Jake not pretending
0 - ∅ Jake
        ∅ pretending

Just for Fun!

Think about the stories you just read. Then draw your favorite part of one of the stories. If you want, you may write to tell about your drawing.

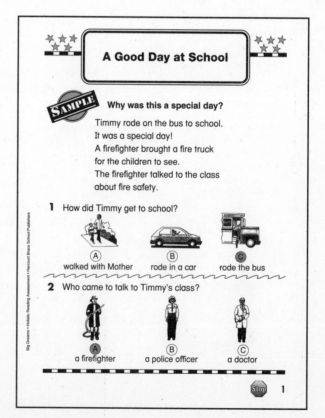

A Good Day at School

SAMPLE

Why was this a special day?

Timmy rode on the bus to school.
It was a special day!
A firefighter brought a fire truck
for the children to see.
The firefighter talked to the class
about fire safety.

1 How did Timmy get to school?

Ⓐ walked with Mother   Ⓑ rode in a car   Ⓒ rode the bus

2 Who came to talk to Timmy's class?

Ⓐ a firefighter   Ⓑ a police officer   Ⓒ a doctor

Harcourt Brace School Publishers • Holistic Reading Assessment

Including DRAGONS

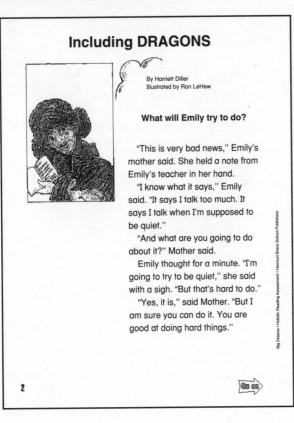

By Harriett Diller
Illustrated by Ron LeHew

What will Emily try to do?

"This is very bad news," Emily's mother said. She held a note from Emily's teacher in her hand.

"I know what it says," Emily said. "It says I talk too much. It says I talk when I'm supposed to be quiet."

"And what are you going to do about it?" Mother said.

Emily thought for a minute. "I'm going to try to be quiet," she said with a sigh. "But that's hard to do."

"Yes, it is," said Mother. "But I am sure you can do it. You are good at doing hard things."

2   Go on →

---

1 Why did Emily get in trouble at school?

(A) talked too much   (B) played with a ball   (C) went to sleep

Go on →   3

Emily wasn't sure she could do it. Being quiet sounded awfully boring. "But what if a lady from outer space lands right next to my desk?" Emily asked. "What if she asks me to tell her all about Earth?"

"Then what will you do, Emily?" asked Mother.

"I'll say, My lips are sealed. I'll say, Talk to me after class."

"I see," said Mother.

"But what if a man says he'll give me a million dollars if I tell him what happened on my favorite TV show last night?"

"Then what will you do, Emily?" asked Mother.

"I'll say, I'll tell you all about it. At recess."

"Good idea," said Mother.

4   Go on →

---

2 What will Emily do if a lady from outer space asks her to talk?

(A) run away   (B) not talk   (C) not hear

Go on →   5

"And if a dragon comes in my class and says he'll breathe fire on anybody who won't talk to him . . ."

Mother's eyes grew wide. "Then what will you do, Emily?"

Emily smiled. "I'll just say, Listen, Dragon. I cannot talk to anybody, dragons included, during class. But I'll talk to you at lunch."

"That will be hard to do," Mother said.

"Sure," said Emily. "But I can do it. I'm good at doing hard things."

"I'll talk to you at lunch."

6   **Go on**

---

3   Who does Emily say she will talk to at lunch?

Ⓐ   Ⓑ   Ⓒ

a dog   an elephant   a dragon

Go on   7

---

4   What do you think Emily will do if a friend talks to her in class?

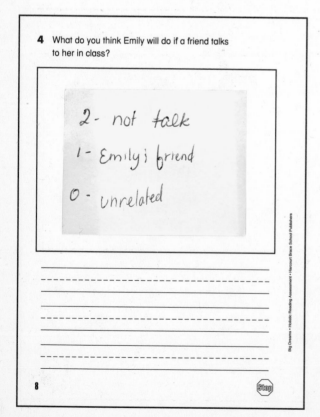

2 - not talk

1 - Emily's friend

0 - unrelated

8   **Stop**

Sara at the Library

By Betty Porter
Illustrated by Meryl Henderson

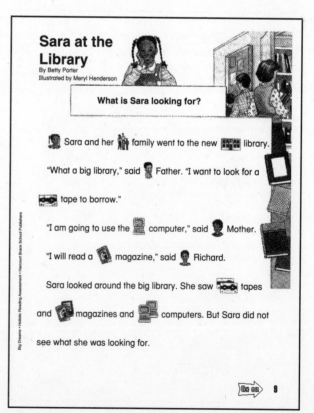

What is Sara looking for?

Sara and her 👪 family went to the new 🏛 library.

"What a big library," said 👨 Father. "I want to look for a 📼 tape to borrow."

"I am going to use the 💻 computer," said 👩 Mother.

"I will read a 📖 magazine," said 👦 Richard.

Sara looked around the big library. She saw 📼 tapes and 📖 magazines and 💻 computers. But Sara did not see what she was looking for.

Go on 9

Harcourt Brace School Publishers • Holistic Reading Assessment

Big Dreams • Holistic Reading Assessment • Harcourt Brace School Publishers

5 Where did Sara and her family go?

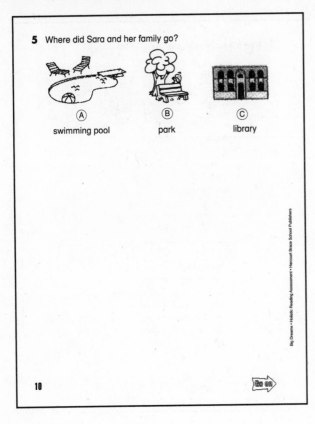

Ⓐ swimming pool   Ⓑ park   Ⓒ library

Go on

Finally she asked a 🧑 librarian for help. The librarian led 📚 Sara into a room with bright 📕 pillows on the floor. Sara smiled. She saw what she was looking for—lots and lots of 📚 books. "Now I can read!" she said, pulling a 📖 book from a 📗 bookshelf. Sara sat down on a 📕 pillow and read her library book.

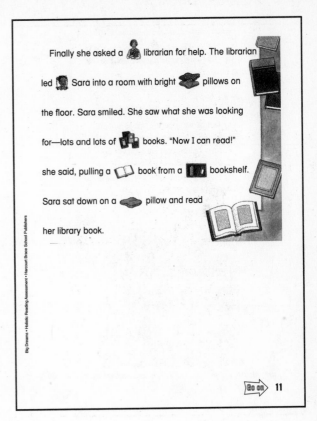

Go on **11**

---

6 Who helped Sara find what she was looking for?

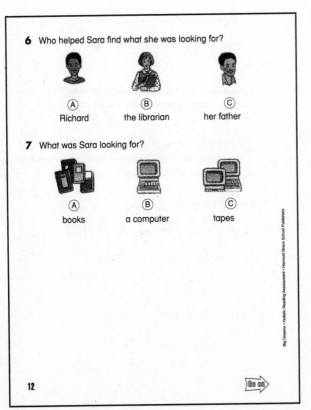

Ⓐ Richard   Ⓑ the librarian   Ⓒ her father

7 What was Sara looking for?

Ⓐ books   Ⓑ a computer   Ⓒ tapes

Go on

---

8 What did Sara do after she found what she wanted?

2 - reading books

1 - Sara w/ library stuff

6 - unrelated

A Good Day at School

SAMPLE

Why was this a special day?

Timmy rode on the bus to school.
It was a special day!
A firefighter brought a fire truck
for the children to see.
The firefighter talked to the class
about fire safety.

1 How did Timmy get to school?

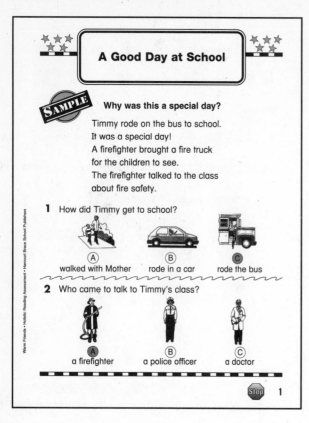

(A) walked with Mother   (B) rode in a car   (C) rode the bus

2 Who came to talk to Timmy's class?

(A) a firefighter   (B) a police officer   (C) a doctor

Stop 1

Turtle Takes Her Time

"Hurry home, Turtle!
A storm is coming."

by Peggy King Anderson
Illustrated by
Liisa Chauncy Guida

Why were all the animals in a hurry?

"Hurry! Hurry home," said Rat.
"A storm is coming." He scurried
down his hole.

Turtle plodded along the
river trail. She moved her
head from side to side,
smelling the river grass.

"Hurry! Hurry home," said
Skunk. "A storm is coming."
She scampered quickly around
Turtle and into the bushes.

Turtle moseyed along.
Eucalyptus leaves twirled
above her head in the
whistling breeze.

2   **Go on**

---

1 Why were Rat and Skunk in a hurry?

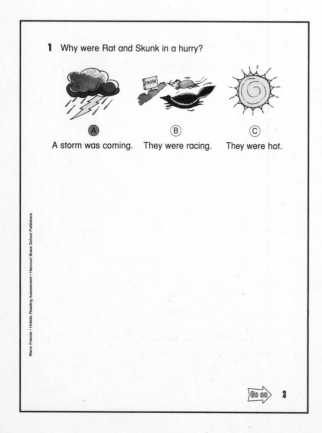

(A) A storm was coming.   (B) They were racing.   (C) They were hot.

Go on 3

"Hurry! Hurry home," said
Muskrat. "A storm is coming."
He swam under the bridge to
his brushy home.

Turtle wandered through the
sedge grass, feeling the spray
from the pond as the wind
whipped it up.

Puffy black clouds surged over Turtle's
head. The bushes snapped back and forth
in the wind.

"Hurry! Hurry home," said
Beaver as he thwacked his
big tail on the water. "A storm
is coming."

Lightning flashed, and
thunder rumbled in the black
clouds over the meadow.

4   **Go on**

Warm Friends • Holistic Reading Assessment • Harcourt Brace School Publishers

Harcourt Brace School Publishers • Holistic Reading Assessment

2 Where did Muskrat go?

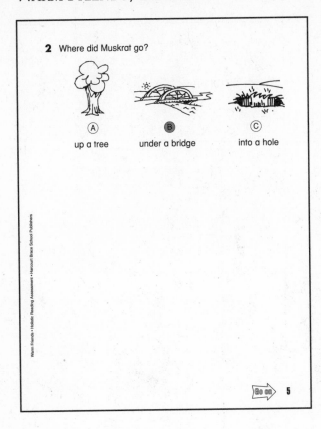

Ⓐ up a tree   Ⓑ under a bridge   Ⓒ into a hole

Go on **5**

"Too late, too late!" said Beaver. "The storm is here."

Beaver ducked under the bulrushes and swam to his lodge.

Big drops of rain splashed down on the pond. The raindrops splashed on the river path, and on the bushes and grass in the meadow.

The raindrops bounced off Turtle's shell.

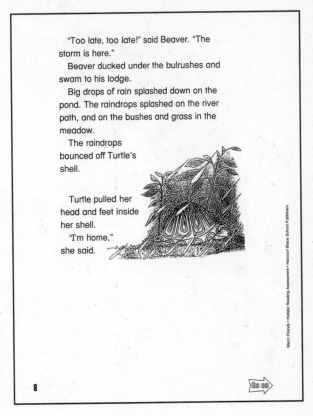

Turtle pulled her head and feet inside her shell.

"I'm home," she said.

6   Go on

---

3 Which animal did <u>not</u> have to hurry home?

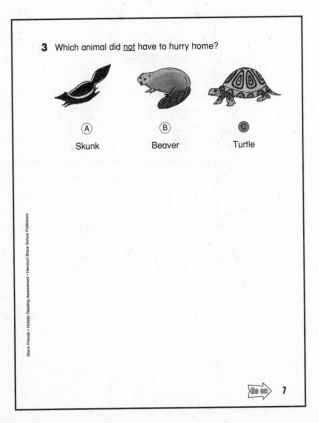

Ⓐ Skunk   Ⓑ Beaver   Ⓒ Turtle

Go on **7**

---

4 What did Turtle do when the storm came?

8   Stop

The Noisy Cat

By Herma Silverstein and Nancy Miller
Illustrated by Suzanne DeMarco

How do Danny and his father help the birds?

Danny and Father hung the new bird feeder in the tree. "Now we will put birdseed in the bird feeder," Father said.

"Oh, no!" Danny cried. "Muffin is climbing the tree. She will try to catch the birds."

"We must think of a way to warn the birds when Muffin is near, so they can fly away," said Father.

Go on 9

5 What do Danny and his father hang in the tree?

Ⓐ a ribbon   Ⓑ a bell   Ⓒ a bird feeder

6 Who does Danny think will hurt the birds?

Ⓐ Muffin   Ⓑ Father   Ⓒ a dog

10

Danny thought hard. Then he ran to get a bell and a ribbon from his toy box.

"The bell will make Muffin noisy, so the birds will know when she is near," Danny said.

Father lifted Muffin down from the tree.

Danny tied the bell to Muffin's collar.

Muffin ran back up the tree. The bell jingled.

"It worked!" said Danny. "Now the birds are safe."

Go on 11

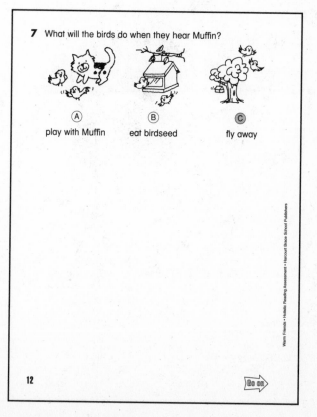

7 What will the birds do when they hear Muffin?

Ⓐ play with Muffin   Ⓑ eat birdseed   Ⓒ fly away

12

Go on

Harcourt Brace School Publishers • Holistic Reading Assessment

8 How will the birds know when Muffin is near?

_____
_____
_____
_____
_____

13

Good Friends

SAMPLE

What do Ben and Jill want to do?

Ben and Jill are good friends. They
play together every day.
One day Ben said, "I want to play ball."
Jill said, "I want to ride bikes."
Ben's father said, "You two can play
ball now, and then go for a bike ride."
"I will play ball with you," said Father.

1 Ben wants to _____.

Ⓐ ride bikes   Ⓑ look at TV   Ⓒ play ball

2 Who will play with Ben and Jill?

Ⓐ Mother   Ⓑ Father   Ⓒ the dog

Stop **1**

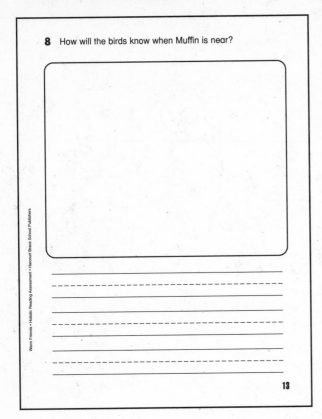

Ma Ma Hu Hu

By Cindy Rogers
Illustrated by Ethel Gold

How does Ali Wong choose a pet?

Ali Wong is sad. His pet white mouse has

died. His friend Ding Li stops by to play. "How are

you today, Ali?" he asks in Chinese.

Ali shrugs and says, *"Ma ma hu hu."* In Chinese, that

means "not too good and not too bad."

Ding says, "Let's visit the animals at the

pet store."

"OK," says Ali. Off they go.

2   Go on ▷

"What do you think of this kitten?" asks Ding.

Ali looks at the kitten. He shrugs and says,

"Ma ma hu hu."

"Well, how about these fine fish?" asks Ding.

Ali looks at the fish and shrugs. *"Ma ma hu hu."*

"How do you like this white mouse?" asks Ding.

Ali looks at the mouse. *"Ma ma hu hu,"* he

finally says.

A parrot ruffles its feathers. "How are you,

pretty parrot?" asks Ding.

"Ma ma hu hu," warbles the parrot.

Ali laughs. "That is a fine pet for

me!" he says.

Go on ▷ **3**

1 How does Ali feel at the beginning of this story?

Ⓐ happy   Ⓑ sad   Ⓒ angry

2 Ali and Ding go to the _____.

Ⓐ school   Ⓑ bank   Ⓒ pet store

3 Who makes Ali laugh and smile?

Ⓐ the mouse   Ⓑ a parrot   Ⓒ Ding Li

4

Go on ⇨

4 What Pet does Ali choose?

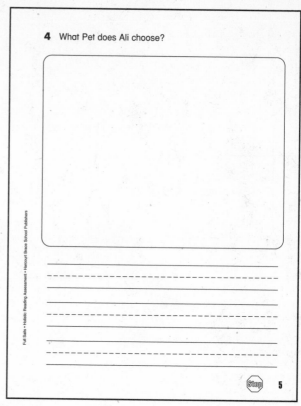

_____

_____

_____

_____

_____

Stop   5

Surprise!
by Arielle North Olson
Art by Jada Rowland

Who will go home with the little girl?

You'll be proud of me, Mom.
Every animal in the pet shop
wanted me to take it home, but . . .
I said no to the rabbit
with the soft white fur.

I said no the puppy
with the big brown eyes.

I said no to the
little gray kitten.

6

Go on ⇨

It was hard, Mom, but . . .
I said no to the parrot
with the long green tail.

I said no the mice
with the tiny pink feet.

I said no to the
little red starfish.

⇨ Go on   7

Harcourt Brace School Publishers • Holistic Reading Assessment

I wanted every one, Mom, but . . .
I said no to the canary
with the bright yellow feathers.

I said no to the fish
with the pretty blue scales.

I said no to the
little black gerbil.

8

Go on

They were so cute, I knew
someone else would buy them.
But . . . SURPRISE!
I said yes to this big old snake.
He looked as if he needed a friend.

Go on 9

5 Where had the little girl been?

A
to a pet shop

B
to the park

C
to her school

6 Which animal had a long green tail?

A
the starfish

B
a mouse

C
the parrot

7 Which animal needed a friend?

A
the snake

B
the gerbil

C
the fish

10

Go on

8 Which animal from the story would you have taken home?

Stop 11

T43

Just for Fun!

Think about the stories you just read. Then draw your favorite part of one of the stories. If you want, you may write to tell about your drawing.

12

13

★★★ **Good Friends** ★★★

SAMPLE

What do Ben and Jill want to do?

Ben and Jill are good friends. They play together every day.
One day Ben said, "I want to play ball."
Jill said, "I want to ride bikes."
Ben's father said, "You two can play ball now, and then go for a bike ride."
"I will play ball with you," said Father.

1 Ben wants to _____.
   (A) ride bikes
   (B) look at TV
   (C) play ball

2 Who will play with Ben and Jill?
   (A) Mother
   (B) Father
   (C) the dog

Stop 1

Shopping

by Sandy Lanton
Art by Tord Nygren

What happens to Becky at lunchtime?

Becky and her mom went shopping on Main Street. Their first stop was the bakery. Mom bought ONE loaf of rye bread. The bakery lady gave Becky a crunchy cookie.
"Thank you," said Becky.
Their second stop was the deli. Mom bought TWO kinds of salads. The deli man gave Becky a sour pickle.
"Mmmm," said Becky.
Their third stop was the butcher shop. Mom bought THREE kinds of meat. The butcher gave Becky a slice of salami.

2

Go on

"Yum," said Becky.

Their fourth stop was the cheese store. Mom bought FOUR kinds of cheese. The cheese lady gave Becky a chunk of cheddar cheese.

"Thanks," said Becky.

Their fifth stop was the fruit stand. Mom bought FIVE different kinds of fruit. The fruit man gave Becky a purple plum.

"Yummy," said Becky.

Then they went home.

"Lunchtime," said Mom.

"LUNCH?" said Becky.

3

1 What were Becky and her mom doing?

- (A) going for a ride
- (B) baking cookies
- (C) shopping

2 How did Becky feel when people gave her things to eat.

- (A) happy
- (B) angry
- (C) sad

3 Why didn't Becky want any lunch?

- (A) She was sleepy.
- (B) She was full.
- (C) She wanted to play.

4

4 What did mom buy the most of?

5

Elephants Should Not Climb Trees

By Jeffie Ross Gordon
Illustrated by Jody Taylor

What happened to Elephant?

"I want to do something new," said Elephant. "I want to climb a tree."

Elephant shook a small tree with his trunk. "But not this tree," he said. "This tree is too small."

6

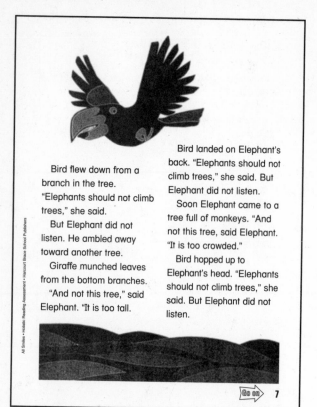

Bird flew down from a branch in the tree. "Elephants should not climb trees," she said.

But Elephant did not listen. He ambled away toward another tree.

Giraffe munched leaves from the bottom branches.

"And not this tree," said Elephant. "It is too tall.

Bird landed on Elephant's back. "Elephants should not climb trees," she said. But Elephant did not listen.

Soon Elephant came to a tree full of monkeys. "And not this tree, said Elephant. "It is too crowded."

Bird hopped up to Elephant's head. "Elephants should not climb trees," she said. But Elephant did not listen.

Go on 7

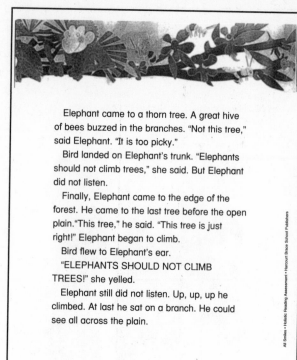

Elephant came to a thorn tree. A great hive of bees buzzed in the branches. "Not this tree," said Elephant. "It is too picky."

Bird landed on Elephant's trunk. "Elephants should not climb trees," she said. But Elephant did not listen.

Finally, Elephant came to the edge of the forest. He came to the last tree before the open plain. "This tree," he said. "This tree is just right!" Elephant began to climb.

Bird flew to Elephant's ear.

"ELEPHANTS SHOULD NOT CLIMB TREES!" she yelled.

Elephant still did not listen. Up, up, up he climbed. At last he sat on a branch. He could see all across the plain.

8

Go on

Bird soared to the top of the tree. She landed beside Elephant. "Elephants should not climb trees," she said.

"Why?" asked Elephant. "WHY should elephants not climb trees?"

"Because elephants cannot get down," said Bird. And she flew away.

Go on 9

---

5 What did Elephant want to do?
(A) go swimming
(B) climb a tree
(C) fly like a bird

6 The tree with the monkeys was too _____ .
(A) crowded
(B) tall
(C) small

7 What does Bird keep telling Elephant?
(A) to stay away from bees
(B) not to climb trees
(C) not to eat leaves

10

Go on

Harcourt Brace School Publishers • Holistic Reading Assessment

8 What happened to Elephant at the end of the story?

Stop **11**

Just for Fun!

Think about the stories you just read. Then draw your favorite part of one of the stories. If you want, you may write to tell about your drawing.

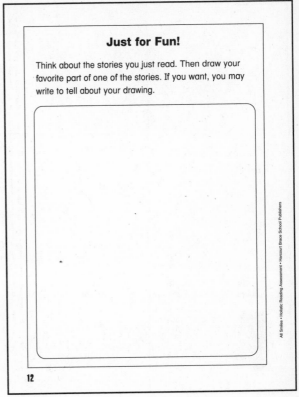

12

13

Harcourt Brace School Publishers • Holistic Reading Assessment

ANSWER KEYS FOR THE HOLISTIC READING ASSESSMENTS

Rhythm and Rhyme/Book K/1

PASSAGE:
Maxie and the Taxi

MULTIPLE-CHOICE ANSWERS:
1. B   2. A   3. C

OPEN-ENDED QUESTION 4:
What did Maxie and the people do at the end of the story?

Score of 2: A Correct Answer
The picture should show Maxie and the people sleeping. This picture may also show the taxi sleeping.

Score of 1: A Partially Correct Answer
The picture may show characters from the story (e.g., Maxie, the people, the taxi) and possibly the setting (i.e., the farm), but does not show anyone sleeping.

Score of 0: An Incorrect Answer
The picture does not show any characters from the story. The response is unresponsive to the question.

PASSAGE:
Walking Through the Forest

MULTIPLE-CHOICE ANSWERS:
5. A   6. C   7. B

OPEN-ENDED QUESTION 8:
What was one of the animals the children wanted to follow them?

Score of 2: A Correct Answer
The picture should show an owl, a squirrel, a fox or a crow (several of the animals may be included). The picture may also show the animal(s) following the children.

Score of 1: A Partially Correct Answer
The picture may show some animals, but they do not seem to be ones that are included in the story. There may be an indication that these animals are following the children.

Score of 0: An Incorrect Answer
The picture does not include any animals from the story, and there is no indication they are following the children. The picture is clearly unresponsive to the question.

Picture Perfect/**Book 1**

PASSAGE:
On Mother's Day

MULTIPLE-CHOICE ANSWERS:
  1. B   2. A   3. C

OPEN-ENDED QUESTION 4:
What gift do you think the children gave their mother?

Score of 2: A Correct Answer
The picture should show presents that the children may have given to Mother. The presents might include flowers, cards, breakfast, or other gifts not mentioned in the story that are appropriate.

Score of 1: A Partially Correct Answer
The picture may include children and Mother, but there will be no indication of any gifts the children have given to Mother.

Score of 0: An Incorrect Answer
The picture does not include any gifts, nor does it include the children or Mother. The picture is clearly unrelated to the question.

PASSAGE:
Now What Am I?

MULTIPLE-CHOICE ANSWERS:
  5. A   6. B   7. C

OPEN-ENDED QUESTION 8:
What was Jake pretending to be in the story?

Score of 2: A Correct Answer
The picture should be of a tree, a bird (blue jay), or an airplane. It could also be a picture of Jake pretending to be one of those things by using his arms and hands as indicated in the story.

Score of 1: A Partially Correct Answer
The picture may be a picture of Jake, but it may not be clear that he is pretending to be any of the three things (tree, blue jay, or airplane).

Score of 0: An Incorrect Answer
The picture does not include any of the three things Jake was pretending to be, nor does it include a picture of Jake pretending to be any of those three things. The picture is unresponsive to the question.

Harcourt Brace School Publishers • Holistic Reading Assessment

T50

Big Dreams/Book 2

PASSAGE:
Including Dragons

MULTIPLE-CHOICE ANSWERS:
1. A   2. B   3. C

OPEN-ENDED QUESTION 4:
What do you think Emily will do if a friend talks to her in class?

Score of 2: A Correct Answer
The response should show Emily with her hands over her mouth or with her mouth shut, or should in some way indicate that Emily will not talk.

Score of 1: A Partially Correct Answer
The response may show Emily alone or Emily with a friend or any character from the story but will not show awareness that Emily will not talk in class.

Score of 0: An Incorrect Answer
The response does not show any characters from the story. It is not clear that the picture is related to the story or the question.

PASSAGE:
Sara at the Library

MULTIPLE-CHOICE ANSWERS:
5. C   6. B   7. A

OPEN-ENDED QUESTION 8:
What did Sara do after she found what she wanted?

Score of 2: A Correct Answer
The response should show Sara reading a book or books.

Score of 1: A Partially Correct Answer
The response may show Sara and books on a shelf, with no indication that she is reading. They may also show Sara with tapes or a computer or any other detail from the story.

Score of 0: An Incorrect Answer
The response does not show any characters or items from the story. It is not clear that the picture is related to the story or the question.

Harcourt Brace School Publishers • Holistic Reading Assessment

Warm Friends/Book 3

PASSAGE:

Turtle Takes Her Time

MULTIPLE-CHOICE ANSWERS:
1. A   2. B   3. C

OPEN-ENDED QUESTION 4:
What did Turtle do when the storm came?

Score of 2: A Correct Answer
The response should show the turtle's shell with no head or feet sticking out. The response may or may not include details about the storm but should show awareness that the turtle was inside her shell.

Score of 1: A Partially Correct Answer
The response may show the turtle or some other character or detail from the story. It will not, however, indicate awareness that the turtle is inside her shell.

Score of 0: An Incorrect Answer
The response does not show any characters or items from the story. It is not clear that the picture is related to the story or the question.

PASSAGE:

The Noisy Cat

MULTIPLE-CHOICE ANSWERS:
5. C   6. A   7. C

OPEN-ENDED QUESTION 8:
How will the birds know when Muffin is near?

Score of 2: A Correct Answer
The response should show a bell or a cat wearing a bell.

Score of 1: A Partially Correct Answer
The response may show a cat or a bird or some other story character or detail but will not show a bell.

Score of 0: An Incorrect Answer
The response does not show any character or item from the story. It is not clear that the picture is related to the story or the question.

Harcourt Brace School Publishers • Holistic Reading Assessment

Full Sails/Book 4

PASSAGE:
Ma Ma Hu Hu

MULTIPLE-CHOICE ANSWERS:
1. B   2. C   3. B

OPEN-ENDED QUESTION 4:
What pet does Ali choose?

Score of 2: A Correct Answer
The response should show a parrot. Ali Wong may or may not be in the picture.

Score of 1: A Partially Correct Answer
The response may show Ali Wong, Ding Li, or the parrot along with other animals. It will not be clear that Ali Wong chose only the parrot for his pet.

Score of 0: An Incorrect Answer
The response does not show any characters or animals from the story. It is not clear that the picture is related to the story or the question.

PASSAGE:
Surprise!

MULTIPLE-CHOICE ANSWERS:
5. A   6. C   7. A

OPEN-ENDED QUESTION 8:
What animal from the story would you have taken home?

Score of 2: A Correct Answer
The response should show an animal from the story.

Score of 1: A Partially Correct Answer
The response may show just the little girl, just the mother, or an animal not mentioned in the story.

Score of 0: An Incorrect Answer
The response does not show any characters or animals from the story. It is not clear that the picture is related to the story or the question.

All Smiles/Book 5

Harcourt Brace School Publishers • Holistic Reading Assessment

PASSAGE:
Shopping

MULTIPLE-CHOICE ANSWERS:
1. C   2. A   3. B

OPEN-ENDED QUESTION 4:
What did mom buy the most of?

Score of 2: A Correct Answer
The response should show some type of fruit.

Score of 1: A Partially Correct Answer
The response may show something else from the story or something to eat, but no fruit.

Score of 0: An Incorrect Answer
The response does not show any characters or items from the story. It is not clear that the picture is related to the story or the question.

PASSAGE:
Elephants Should Not Climb Trees

MULTIPLE-CHOICE ANSWERS:
5. B   6. A   7. B

OPEN-ENDED QUESTION 8:
What happened to Elephant at the end of the story?

Score of 2: A Correct Answer
The response should show Elephant somewhere in or on a tree.

Score of 1: A Partially Correct Answer
The response may show a tree, but will not indicate understanding that the elephant could not get down from the tree. Responses may also show any other character or detail from the story.

Score of 0: An Incorrect Answer
The response does not show any characters or items from the story. It is not clear that the picture is related to the story or the question.

Signatures

HOLISTIC READING ASSESSMENT

CLASS RECORD FORM

Teacher _____

School _____

Student Name	BOOK K/1		BOOK 1		BOOK 2	
	Total Score	Date_____ Comments	Total Score	Date_____ Comments	Total Score	Date_____ Comments

HOLISTIC READING ASSESSMENT

CLASS RECORD FORM

Signatures

Teacher _____

School _____

Student Name	BOOK 3		BOOK 4		BOOK 5	
	Total Score	Date___ Comments	Total Score	Date___ Comments	Total Score	Date___ Comments

Harcourt Brace School Publishers • Holistic Reading Assessment

Signatures

HOLISTIC READING ASSESSMENT
RHYTHM AND RHYME/BOOK K/1

Summary of Performance

Name _____ **Grade** _____ **Date** _____

Passage 1	*Pupil Score*	*Comments*
Multiple Choice (1–3)	_____	_____
Open-ended (4)	_____	_____

Passage 2	*Pupil Score*	*Comments*
Multiple Choice (5–7)	_____	_____
Open-ended (8)	_____	_____
Total Score	_____	_____

Performance Level

Very Good Reader	*Average Reader*	*Fair Reader*	*Limited Reader*
9–10	7–8	5–6	Fewer than 5

For permission to reprint copyrighted material, grateful acknowledgment is
made to the following sources:

Toni Goffe: Illustrations by Toni Goffe from "Maxie and the Taxi" by Dennis Lee
in *Ladybug* Magazine, November 1994.

LADYBUG Magazine: "Walking Through the Forest" by Shelee C. O'Dell from
Ladybug Magazine, June 1993. Text © 1993 by Shelee C. O'Dell.

Sterling Lord Associates: "Maxie and the Taxi" by Dennis Lee from *Ladybug*
Magazine, November 1994. Text © 1991 by Dennis Lee.

Publishers' Graphics, Inc.: Illustrations by Joan Holub from "Walking Through
the Forest" by Shelee C. O'Dell in *Ladybug* Magazine, June 1993.

Printed in the United States of America

ISBN 0-15-308238-0

1 2 3 4 5 6 7 8 9 10   022   99   98   97   96

A Good Day at School

Why was this a special day?

Timmy rode on the bus to school.
It was a special day!
A firefighter brought a fire truck
for the children to see.
The firefighter talked to the class
about fire safety.

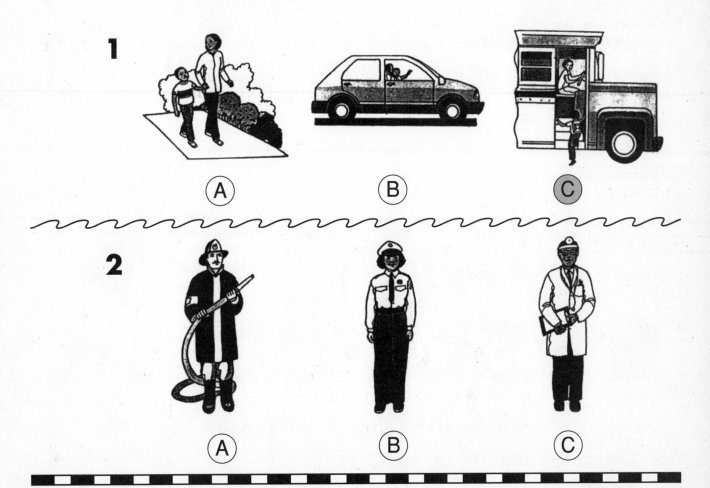

1

Ⓐ　　　　Ⓑ　　　　Ⓒ

2

Ⓐ　　　　Ⓑ　　　　Ⓒ

Stop　1

Maxie and the Taxi

by Dennis Lee • Art by Toni Goffe

What does Maxie do?

Maxie drove a taxi

With a *beep! beep! beep!*

And he picked up all the people
In a heap, heap, heap.

2

Go on

He took them to the farm

To see the sheep, sheep, sheep—

Then, Maxie and the taxi
Went to sleep, sleep, sleep.

Go on

1

Ⓐ   Ⓑ   Ⓒ

2

Ⓐ   Ⓑ   Ⓒ

3

Ⓐ   Ⓑ   Ⓒ

4

Go on ➡

4 What did Maxie and the people do at the end of the story?

5

Walking Through the Forest

An Action Rhyme
by Shelee C. O'Dell • Art by Joan Holub

What did the children see as they walked through the forest?

Walking through
the forest,

What do I see?

A squirrel—flip, flap!

Come and follow me.

Walking through the forest,

What do I see?

A crow—caw, caw!

Come and follow me.

Walking through the forest,

What do I see?

An owl—hoot, hoot!

Come and follow me.

Walking through the forest,

What do I see?

A fox—hehh, hehh, hehh!

Come and follow me.

Walking through the forest,

What do I smell?

A skunk—PEW!

Don't you follow me!

 Go on

5

Ⓐ   Ⓑ   Ⓒ

6

Ⓐ   Ⓑ   Ⓒ

7

Ⓐ   Ⓑ   Ⓒ

8

Rhythm and Rhyme • Holistic Reading Assessment • Harcourt Brace School Publishers

8 What was one of the animals the children wanted to follow them?

Rhythm and Rhyme • Holistic Reading Assessment • Harcourt Brace School Publishers

Just for Fun!

Think about the stories you just read. Then draw your favorite part of one of the stories. If you want, you may write to tell about your drawing.

Rhythm and Rhyme • Holistic Reading Assessment • Harcourt Brace School Publishers

Rhythm and Rhyme • Holistic Reading Assessment • Harcourt Brace School Publishers

Signatures

RHYTHM AND RHYME

HOLISTIC READING ASSESSMENT

HARCOURT BRACE

ORLANDO ATLANTA AUSTIN BOSTON SAN FRANCISCO CHICAGO DALLAS NEW YORK
TORONTO LONDON

PART NO. 9997-17423-2

ISBN 0-15-308238-0 (PACKAGE OF 12)

K/1

Signatures

HOLISTIC READING ASSESSMENT
PICTURE PERFECT/BOOK 1

Summary of Performance

Name _____ Grade _____ Date _____

Passage 1	*Pupil Score*	*Comments*
Multiple Choice (1–3)	_____	_____
Open-ended (4)	_____	_____

Passage 2	*Pupil Score*	*Comments*
Multiple Choice (5–7)	_____	_____
Open-ended (8)	_____	_____
Total Score	_____	_____

Performance Level

Very Good Reader	*Average Reader*	*Fair Reader*	*Limited Reader*
9–10	7–8	5–6	Fewer than 5

For permission to reprint copyrighted material, grateful acknowledgment
is made to the following sources:

Aileen Fisher: "On Mother's Day" from *Skip Around the Year* by Aileen
Fisher. Text © 1967 by Aileen Fisher.

Highlights for Children, Inc., Columbus, OH: "Now What Am I?"
by Diane Burns, illustrated by Meryl Henderson from *Highlights for
Children* Magazine, January 1994. Copyright © 1994 by Highlights for
Children, Inc.

Kirchoff/Wohlberg, Inc.: Illustrations by Kathleen Howell from "On
Mother's Day" by Aileen Fisher in *Ladybug* Magazine, May 1994.

Printed in the United States of America

ISBN 0-15-308239-9

1 2 3 4 5 6 7 8 9 10   022   99   98   97   96

A Good Day at School

Why was this a special day?

Timmy rode on the bus to school.
It was a special day!
A firefighter brought a fire truck
for the children to see.
The firefighter talked to the class
about fire safety.

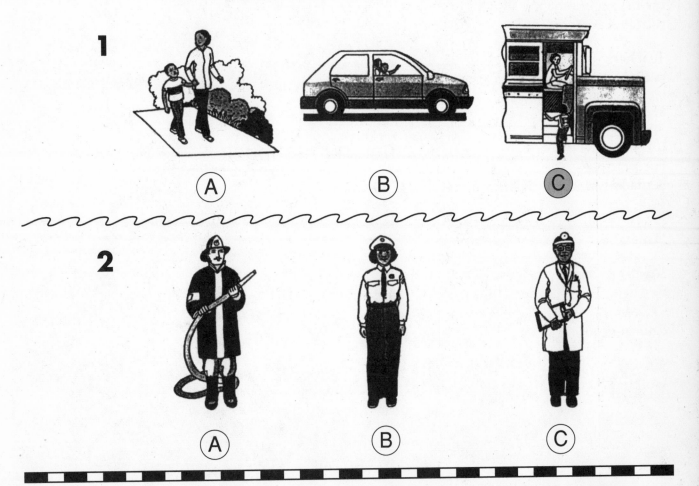

1

Ⓐ   Ⓑ   Ⓒ

2

Ⓐ   Ⓑ   Ⓒ

Picture Perfect • Holistic Reading Assessment • Harcourt Brace School Publishers

On Mother's Day

by Aileen Fisher   Art by Kathleen Howell

What surprise did the children make?

On Mother's Day we got up first
so full of plans we almost burst.

We started breakfast right away
as our surprise for Mother's Day.

We picked some flowers, then hurried back
to make the coffee—rather black.

2

Picture Perfect • Holistic Reading Assessment • Harcourt Brace School Publishers

Ⓐ Ⓑ Ⓒ

Picture Perfect • Holistic Reading Assessment • Harcourt Brace School Publishers

We wrapped our gifts and wrote a card
and boiled the eggs—a little hard.

And then we sang a serenade,
which burned the toast, I am afraid.

But Mother said, amidst our cheers,
"Oh, what a big surprise, my dears,
I've not had such a treat in years."
And she was smiling to her ears!

Picture Perfect • Holistic Reading Assessment • Harcourt Brace School Publishers

2

A   B   C

3

A   B   C

4   What gift do you think the children gave their mother?

Picture Perfect • Holistic Reading Assessment • Harcourt Brace School Publishers

Picture Perfect • Holistic Reading Assessment • Harcourt Brace School Publishers

7

Now What Am I?

by Diane Burns

Illustrated by Meryl Henderson

What was Jake pretending to be?

"Look, Dad," said Jake. "Can you guess what I

am?" Jake flapped his arms and said, "Jay, jay!"

"You are a blue jay, Dad guessed.

"Yes," Jake said. "Can you guess this?" He held his

arms up high. He wiggled his fingers. He whispered,

"Rustle, rustle, rustle."

"Are you a  tree?" guessed Dad.

"Yes," said Jake.

Picture Perfect • Holistic Reading Assessment • Harcourt Brace School Publishers

5

Picture Perfect • Holistic Reading Assessment • Harcourt Brace School Publishers

He stuck his  arms out sideways. "Now what am

I? Zoom, zoom!"

"An airplane?" guessed Dad.

"Yes. Now I can do something else with my arms,"

 Jake said. He gave Dad a big  hug.

"You must be my Jake again," said Dad.

"Right!" said Jake.

"I am glad," said Dad.

Picture Perfect • Holistic Reading Assessment • Harcourt Brace School Publishers

 Go on

6

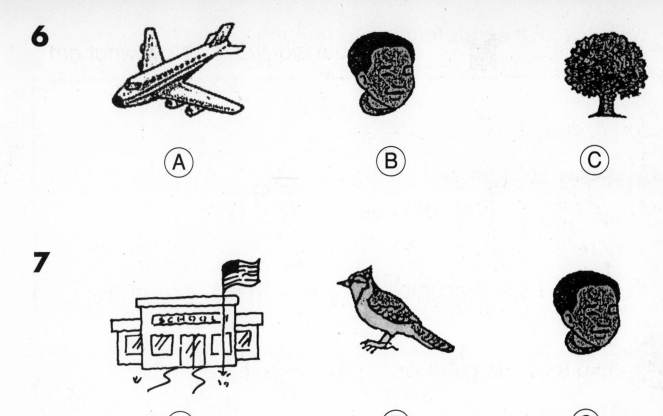

Ⓐ   Ⓑ   Ⓒ

7

Ⓐ   Ⓑ   Ⓒ

8 What was Jake pretending to be in the story?

Picture Perfect • Holistic Reading Assessment • Harcourt Brace School Publishers

Just for Fun!

Think about the stories you just read. Then draw your favorite part of one of the stories. If you want, you may write to tell about your drawing.

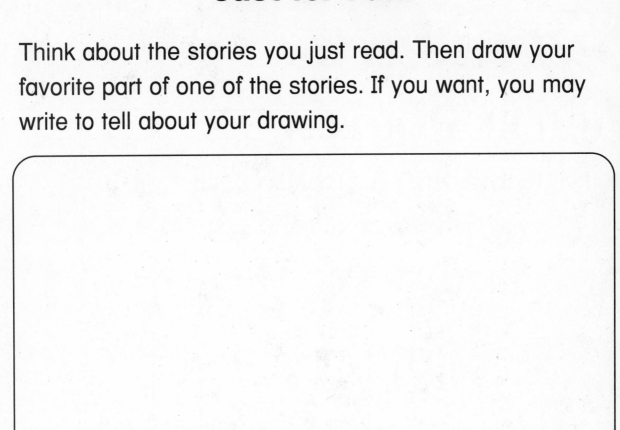

Signatures

PICTURE PERFECT

HOLISTIC READING ASSESSMENT

HARCOURT
BRACE

ORLANDO ATLANTA AUSTIN BOSTON SAN FRANCISCO CHICAGO DALLAS NEW YORK
TORONTO LONDON

PART NO. 9997-17424-0

ISBN 0-15-308239-9 (PACKAGE OF 12)

1-1

Signatures

HOLISTIC READING ASSESSMENT
BIG DREAMS/BOOK 2

Summary of Performance

Name _____ **Grade** _____ **Date** _____

Passage 1	*Pupil Score*	*Comments*
Multiple Choice (1–3)	_____	_____
Open-ended (4)	_____	_____

Passage 2	*Pupil Score*	*Comments*
Multiple Choice (5–7)	_____	_____
Open-ended (8)	_____	_____
Total Score	_____	_____

Performance Level

Very Good Reader	*Average Reader*	*Fair Reader*	*Limited Reader*
9–10	7–8	5–6	Fewer than 5

For permission to reprint copyrighted material, grateful acknowledgment is
made to the following sources:

Boyds Mills Press, Inc.: "Sara at the Library" by Betty Porter, illustrated
by Meryl Henderson from *Rebus Treasury II*, compiled by the editors of
Highlights for Children. Copyright © 1993 by Boyds Mills Press.

Highlights for Children, Inc., Columbus, OH: "Including Dragons" by Harriett
Diller, illustrated by Ron LeHew from *Highlights for Children* Magazine, March
1990. Copyright © 1990 by Highlights for Children, Inc.

Printed in the United States of America

ISBN 0-15-308240-2

1 2 3 4 5 6 7 8 9 10   022   99   98   97   96

A Good Day at School

Why was this a special day?

Timmy rode on the bus to school.
It was a special day!
A firefighter brought a fire truck
for the children to see.
The firefighter talked to the class
about fire safety.

1 How did Timmy get to school?

Ⓐ
walked with Mother

Ⓑ
rode in a car

Ⓒ
rode the bus

2 Who came to talk to Timmy's class?

Ⓐ
a firefighter

Ⓑ
a police officer

Ⓒ
a doctor

Including DRAGONS

By Harriett Diller
Illustrated by Ron LeHew

What will Emily try to do?

"This is very bad news," Emily's mother said. She held a note from Emily's teacher in her hand.

" I know what it says," Emily said. "It says I talk too much. It says I talk when I'm supposed to be quiet."

"And what are you going to do about it?" Mother said.

Emily thought for a minute. "I'm going to try to be quiet," she said with a sigh. "But that's hard to do."

"Yes, it is," said Mother. "But I am sure you can do it. You are good at doing hard things."

Big Dreams • Holistic Reading Assessment • Harcourt Brace School Publishers

Go on

1 Why did Emily get in trouble at school?

(A) talked too much   (B) played with a ball   (C) went to sleep

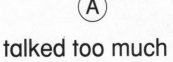
Big Dreams • Holistic Reading Assessment • Harcourt Brace School Publishers

Emily wasn't sure she could do it. Being quiet sounded awfully boring. "But what if a lady from outer space lands right next to my desk?" Emily asked. "What if she asks me to tell her all about Earth?"

"Then what will you do, Emily?" asked Mother.

"I'll say, My lips are sealed. I'll say, Talk to me after class."

"I see," said Mother.

"My lips are sealed."

"But what if a man says he'll give me a million dollars if I tell him what happened on my favorite TV show last night?"

"Then what will you do, Emily?" asked Mother.

"I'll say, I'll tell you all about it. At recess."

"Good idea," said Mother.

"I'll tell you at recess."

Big Dreams • Holistic Reading Assessment • Harcourt Brace School Publishers

Go on

2 What will Emily do if a lady from outer space
asks her to talk?

Ⓐ

run away

Ⓑ

not talk

Ⓒ

not hear

"And if a dragon comes in my class and says he'll breathe fire on anybody who won't talk to him . . ."

Mother's eyes grew wide. "Then what will you do, Emily?"

Emily smiled. "I'll just say, Listen, Dragon. I cannot talk to anybody, dragons included, during class. But I'll talk to you at lunch."

"That will be hard to do," Mother said.

"Sure," said Emily. "But I can do it. I'm good at doing hard things."

Big Dreams • Holistic Reading Assessment • Harcourt Brace School Publishers

3   Who does Emily say she will talk to at lunch?

Ⓐ

a dog

Ⓑ

an elephant

Ⓒ

a dragon

4 What do you think Emily will do if a friend talks to her in class?

Big Dreams • Holistic Reading Assessment • Harcourt Brace School Publishers

Sara at the Library

By Betty Porter

Illustrated by Meryl Henderson

What is Sara looking for?

 Sara and her family went to the new library.

"What a big library," said Father. "I want to look for a

 tape to borrow."

"I am going to use the computer," said Mother.

"I will read a magazine," said Richard.

Sara looked around the big library. She saw tapes

and magazines and computers. But Sara did not

see what she was looking for.

Big Dreams • Holistic Reading Assessment • Harcourt Brace School Publishers

5 Where did Sara and her family go?

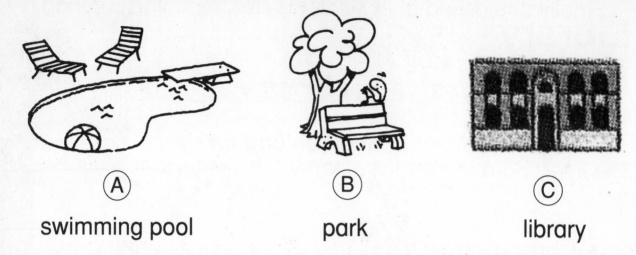

Ⓐ swimming pool

Ⓑ park

Ⓒ library

Big Dreams • Holistic Reading Assessment • Harcourt Brace School Publishers

Go on

Finally she asked a librarian for help. The librarian

led Sara into a room with bright pillows on

the floor. Sara smiled. She saw what she was looking

for—lots and lots of   books. "Now I can read!"

she said, pulling a book from a bookshelf.

Sara sat down on a pillow and read

her library book.

Go on

6 Who helped Sara find what she was looking for?

Ⓐ
Richard

Ⓑ
the librarian

Ⓒ
her father

7 What was Sara looking for?

Ⓐ
books

Ⓑ
a computer

Ⓒ
tapes

Big Dreams • Holistic Reading Assessment • Harcourt Brace School Publishers

Go on

8 What did Sara do after she found what she wanted?

Big Dreams • Holistic Reading Assessment • Harcourt Brace School Publishers

Signatures

Big Dreams

Holistic Reading Assessment

HARCOURT
BRACE

ORLANDO ATLANTA AUSTIN BOSTON SAN FRANCISCO CHICAGO DALLAS NEW YORK
TORONTO LONDON

PART NO. 9997-17425-9

ISBN 0-15-308240-2 (PACKAGE OF 12)

1-2

Signatures

HOLISTIC READING ASSESSMENT

WARM FRIENDS/BOOK 3

Summary of Performance

Name _____ **Grade** _____ **Date** _____

Passage 1	*Pupil Score*	*Comments*
Multiple Choice (1–3)	_____	_____
Open-ended (4)	_____	_____

Passage 2	*Pupil Score*	*Comments*
Multiple Choice (5–7)	_____	_____
Open-ended (8)	_____	_____
Total Score	_____	_____

Performance Level

Very Good Reader	*Average Reader*	*Fair Reader*	*Limited Reader*
9–10	7–8	5–6	Fewer than 5

For permission to reprint copyrighted material, grateful acknowledgment is made to the following source:

Highlights for Children, Inc., Columbus, OH: "Turtle Takes Her Time" by Peggy King Anderson, illustrated by Liisa Chauncy Guida from *Highlights for Children* Magazine, September 1994. Copyright © 1994 by Highlights for Children, Inc. "The Noisy Cat" by Herma Silverstein and Nancy Miller, illustrated by Suzanne DeMarco from *Highlights for Children* Magazine, January 1993. Copyright © 1993 by Highlights for Children, Inc.

Printed in the United States of America

ISBN 0-15-308241-0

1 2 3 4 5 6 7 8 9 10   022   99   98   97   96

A Good Day at School

Why was this a special day?

Timmy rode on the bus to school.
It was a special day!
A firefighter brought a fire truck
for the children to see.
The firefighter talked to the class
about fire safety.

1 How did Timmy get to school?

(A)

walked with Mother

(B)

rode in a car

(C)

rode the bus

2 Who came to talk to Timmy's class?

(A)

a firefighter

(B)

a police officer

(C)

a doctor

Turtle Takes Her Time

"Hurry home, Turtle!
A storm is coming."

by Peggy King Anderson

Illustrated by
Liisa Chauncy Guida

Why were all the animals in a hurry?

"Hurry! Hurry home," said Rat. "A storm is coming." He scurried down his hole.

Turtle plodded along the river trail. She moved her head from side to side, smelling the river grass.

"Hurry! Hurry home," said Skunk. "A storm is coming." She scampered quickly around Turtle and into the bushes.

Turtle moseyed along. Eucalyptus leaves twirled above her head in the whistling breeze.

Warm Friends • Holistic Reading Assessment • Harcourt Brace School Publishers

Go on

1 Why were Rat and Skunk in a hurry?

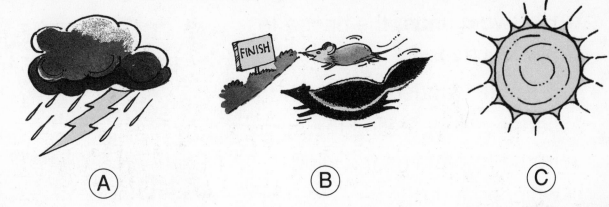

(A) A storm was coming.   (B) They were racing.   (C) They were hot.

"Hurry! Hurry home," said Muskrat. "A storm is coming." He swam under the bridge to his brushy home.

Turtle wandered through the sedge grass, feeling the spray from the pond as the wind whipped it up.

Puffy black clouds surged over Turtle's head. The bushes snapped back and forth in the wind.

"Hurry! Hurry home," said Beaver as he thwacked his big tail on the water. "A storm is coming."

Lightning flashed, and thunder rumbled in the black clouds over the meadow.

4

2 Where did Muskrat go?

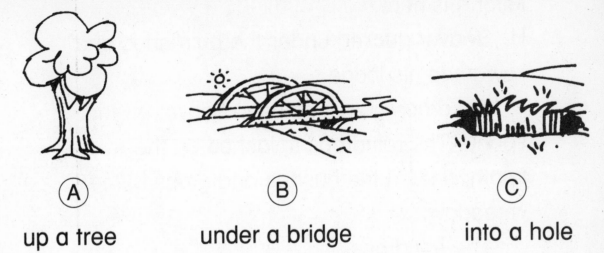

Ⓐ up a tree

Ⓑ under a bridge

Ⓒ into a hole

Warm Friends • Holistic Reading Assessment • Harcourt Brace School Publishers

"Too late, too late!" said Beaver. "The storm is here."

Beaver ducked under the bulrushes and swam to his lodge.

Big drops of rain splashed down on the pond. The raindrops splashed on the river path, and on the bushes and grass in the meadow.

The raindrops bounced off Turtle's shell.

Turtle pulled her head and feet inside her shell.

"I'm home," she said.

6

Warm Friends • Holistic Reading Assessment • Harcourt Brace School Publishers

3 Which animal did <u>not</u> have to hurry home?

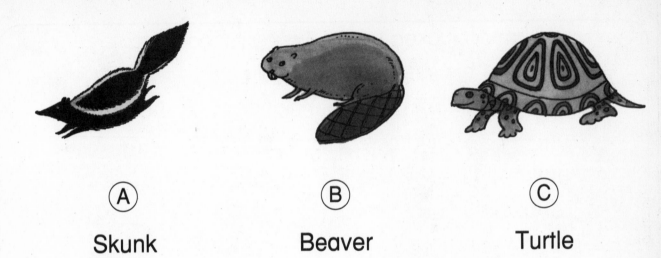

Ⓐ

Skunk

Ⓑ

Beaver

Ⓒ

Turtle

Warm Friends • Holistic Reading Assessment • Harcourt Brace School Publishers

4 What did Turtle do when the storm came?

Warm Friends • Holistic Reading Assessment • Harcourt Brace School Publishers

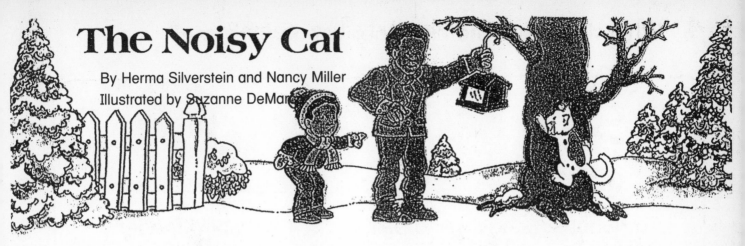

The Noisy Cat

By Herma Silverstein and Nancy Miller

Illustrated by Suzanne DeMar

How do Danny and his father help the birds?

 Danny and Father hung the new bird

feeder in the tree. "Now we will put birdseed in

the bird feeder," Father said.

"Oh, no!" Danny cried. " Muffin is climbing the tree.

She will try to catch the birds."

"We must think of a way to warn the birds when

Muffin is near, so they can fly away," said Father.

5 What do Danny and his father hang in the tree?

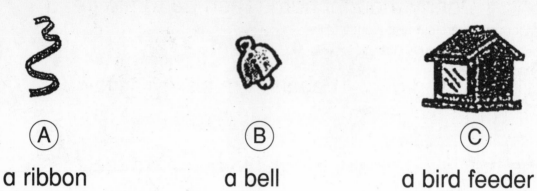

(A) a ribbon

(B) a bell

(C) a bird feeder

6 Who does Danny think will hurt the birds?

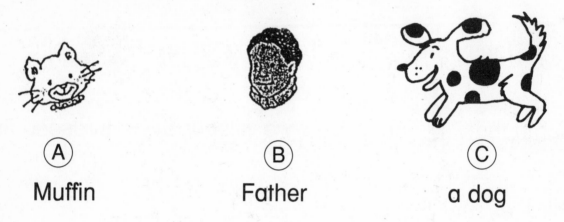

(A) Muffin

(B) Father

(C) a dog

Warm Friends • Holistic Reading Assessment • Harcourt Brace School Publishers

Go on

Danny thought hard. Then he ran to get a

 bell and a ribbon from his toy box.

"The bell will make Muffin noisy, so the

birds will know when she is near," Danny said.

 Father lifted Muffin down from the tree.

Danny tied the bell to Muffin's ⬭ collar.

Muffin ran back up the tree. The bell jingled.

"It worked!" said Danny. "Now the birds are safe."

Warm Friends • Holistic Reading Assessment • Harcourt Brace School Publishers

Go on

7 What will the birds do when they hear Muffin?

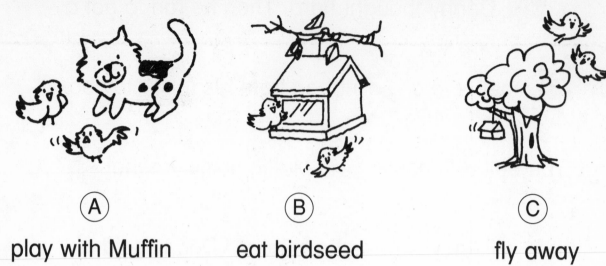

Ⓐ
play with Muffin

Ⓑ
eat birdseed

Ⓒ
fly away

Warm Friends • Holistic Reading Assessment • Harcourt Brace School Publishers

Go on ⟩

8 How will the birds know when Muffin is near?

Warm Friends • Holistic Reading Assessment • Harcourt Brace School Publishers

Signatures

WARM FRIENDS

HOLISTIC READING ASSESSMENT

HARCOURT
BRACE

ORLANDO ATLANTA AUSTIN BOSTON SAN FRANCISCO CHICAGO DALLAS NEW YORK
TORONTO LONDON

PART NO. 9997-17426-7

ISBN 0-15-308241-0 (PACKAGE OF 12)

1-3

Signatures

HOLISTIC READING ASSESSMENT
FULL SAILS/BOOK 4

Summary of Performance

Name _____   Grade _____   Date _____

Passage 1	*Pupil Score*	*Comments*
Multiple Choice (1–3)	_____	_____
Open-ended (4)	_____	_____

Passage 2	*Pupil Score*	*Comments*
Multiple Choice (5–7)	_____	_____
Open-ended (8)	_____	_____
Total Score	_____	_____

Performance Level

Very Good Reader	*Average Reader*	*Fair Reader*	*Limited Reader*
9–10	7–8	5–6	Fewer than 5

For permission to reprint copyrighted material, grateful acknowledgment is made to the following sources:

Curtis Brown Ltd.: "Surprise!" by Arielle North Olson from *Ladybug* Magazine, January 1995. Text copyright © 1995 by Arielle North Olson.

Highlights for Children, Inc., Columbus, OH: "Ma Ma Hu Hu" by Cindy Rogers, illustrated by Ethel Gold from *Highlights for Children* Magazine, May 1994. Copyright © 1994 by Highlights for Children, Inc.

Jada Rowland: Illustrations by Jada Rowland from "Surprise!" by Arielle North Olson in *Ladybug* Magazine, January 1995.

Printed in the United States of America

ISBN 0-15-308242-9

1 2 3 4 5 6 7 8 9 10   022   99   98   97   96

Good Friends

What do Ben and Jill want to do?

Ben and Jill are good friends. They
play together every day.
One day Ben said, "I want to play ball."
Jill said, "I want to ride bikes."
Ben's father said, "You two can play
ball now, and then go for a bike ride."
"I will play ball with you," said Father.

1 Ben wants to _____ .

Ⓐ   Ⓑ   Ⓒ
ride bikes   look at TV   play ball

2 Who will play with Ben and Jill?

Ⓐ   Ⓑ   Ⓒ
Mother   Father   the dog

Ma Ma Hu Hu

By Cindy Rogers
Illustrated by Ethel Gold

How does Ali Wong choose a pet?

 Ali Wong is sad. His pet white mouse has

died. His friend 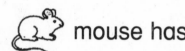 Ding Li stops by to play. "How are

you today, Ali?" he asks in Chinese.

Ali shrugs and says, *"Ma ma hu hu."* In Chinese, that

means "not too good and not too bad."

Ding says, "Let's visit the animals at the

 pet store."

"OK," says Ali. Off they go.

Full Sails • Holistic Reading Assessment • Harcourt Brace School Publishers

Go on

"What do you think of this kitten?" asks Ding.

 Ali looks at the kitten. He shrugs and says,

"Ma ma hu hu."

"Well, how about these fine fish?" asks Ding.

Ali looks at the fish and shrugs. *"Ma ma hu hu."*

"How do you like this white mouse?" asks Ding.

Ali looks at the mouse. *"Ma ma hu hu,"* he

finally says.

A parrot ruffles its  feathers. "How are you,

pretty parrot?" asks Ding.

"Ma ma hu hu," warbles the parrot.

Ali laughs. "That is a fine pet for

me!" he says.

Full Sails • Holistic Reading Assessment • Harcourt Brace School Publishers

1 **How does Ali feel at the beginning of this story?**

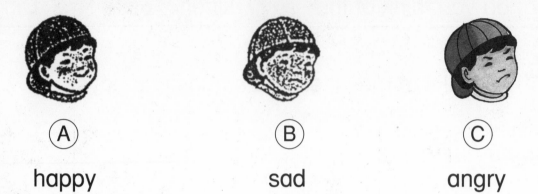

Ⓐ
happy

Ⓑ
sad

Ⓒ
angry

2 Ali and Ding go to the _____ .

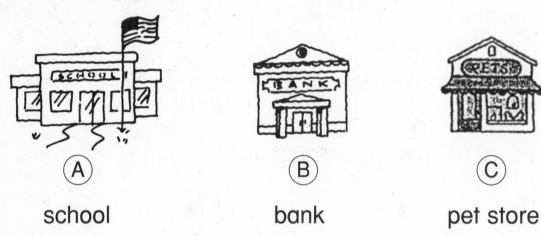

Ⓐ
school

Ⓑ
bank

Ⓒ
pet store

3 **Who makes Ali laugh and smile?**

Ⓐ
the mouse

Ⓑ
a parrot

Ⓒ
Ding Li

4

Full Sails • Holistic Reading Assessment • Harcourt Brace School Publishers

4   What Pet does Ali choose?

Full Sails • Holistic Reading Assessment • Harcourt Brace School Publishers

Surprise!

by Arielle North Olson
Art by Jada Rowland

Who will go home with the little girl?

You'll be proud of me, Mom.
Every animal in the pet shop
wanted me to take it home, but . . .
I said no to the rabbit
with the soft white fur.

I said no the puppy
with the big brown eyes.

I said no to the
little gray kitten.

Go on

It was hard, Mom, but . . .
I said no to the parrot
with the long green tail.

I said no the mice
with the tiny pink feet.

I said no to the
little red starfish.

 Go on

I wanted every one, Mom, but . . .
I said no to the canary
with the bright yellow feathers.

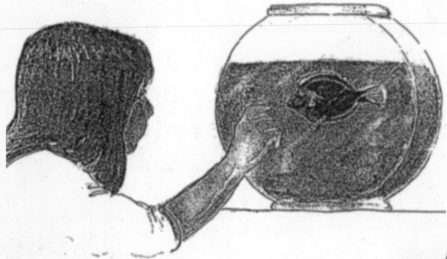

I said no to the fish
with the pretty blue scales.

I said no to the
little black gerbil.

Full Sails • Holistic Reading Assessment • Harcourt Brace School Publishers

They were so cute, I knew
someone else would buy them.
But . . . SURPRISE!
I said yes to this big old snake.
He looked as if he needed a friend.

 Go on

5 Where had the little girl been?

Ⓐ

to a pet shop

Ⓑ

to the park

Ⓒ

to her school

6 Which animal had a long green tail?

Ⓐ

the starfish

Ⓑ

a mouse

Ⓒ

the parrot

7 Which animal needed a friend?

Ⓐ

the snake

Ⓑ

the gerbil

Ⓒ

the fish

10

Full Sails • Holistic Reading Assessment • Harcourt Brace School Publishers

8 Which animal from the story would you have taken home?

Just for Fun!

Think about the stories you just read. Then draw your favorite part of one of the stories. If you want, you may write to tell about your drawing.

Full Sails • Holistic Reading Assessment • Harcourt Brace School Publishers

Full Sails • Holistic Reading Assessment • Harcourt Brace School Publishers

Signatures

FULL SAILS

HOLISTIC READING ASSESSMENT

HARCOURT BRACE

ORLANDO ATLANTA AUSTIN BOSTON SAN FRANCISCO CHICAGO DALLAS NEW YORK
TORONTO LONDON

PART NO. 9997-17427-5

ISBN 0-15-308242-9 (PACKAGE OF 12)

1-4

Signatures

Holistic Reading Assessment
All Smiles/Book 5

Summary of Performance

Name _____ **Grade** _____ **Date** _____

Passage 1	*Pupil Score*	*Comments*
Multiple Choice (1–3)	_____	_____
Open-ended (4)	_____	_____

Passage 2	*Pupil Score*	*Comments*
Multiple Choice (5–7)	_____	_____
Open-ended (8)	_____	_____
Total Score	_____	_____

Performance Level

Very Good Reader	*Average Reader*	*Fair Reader*	*Limited Reader*
9–10	7–8	5–6	Fewer than 5

For permission to reprint copyrighted material, grateful acknowledgment is made to the following sources:

Highlights for Children, Inc., Columbus, OH: "Elephants Should Not Climb Trees" by Jeffie Ross Gordon, illustrated by Jody Taylor from *Highlights for Children* Magazine, July 1994. Copyright © 1994 by Highlights for Children, Inc.

LADYBUG Magazine: "Shopping" by Sandy Lanton from *Ladybug* Magazine, May 1994. Text © 1994 by Sandra Lanton.

Tord Nygren: Illustrations by Tord Nygren from "Shopping" by Sandy Lanton in *Ladybug* Magazine, May 1994.

Printed in the United States of America

ISBN 0-15-308243-7

1 2 3 4 5 6 7 8 9 10   022   99   98   97   96

Good Friends

What do Ben and Jill want to do?

Ben and Jill are good friends. They
play together every day.
One day Ben said, "I want to play ball."
Jill said, "I want to ride bikes."
Ben's father said, "You two can play
ball now, and then go for a bike ride."
"I will play ball with you," said Father.

1 Ben wants to _____.

    Ⓐ ride bikes

    Ⓑ look at TV

    Ⓒ play ball

2 Who will play with Ben and Jill?

    Ⓐ Mother

    Ⓑ Father

    Ⓒ the dog

Shopping

by Sandy Lanton
Art by Tord Nygren

What happens to Becky at lunchtime?

Becky and her mom went shopping on Main Street. Their first stop was the bakery. Mom bought ONE loaf of rye bread. The bakery lady gave Becky a crunchy cookie.

"Thank you," said Becky.

Their second stop was the deli. Mom bought TWO kinds of salads. The deli man gave Becky a sour pickle.

"Mmmm," said Becky.

Their third stop was the butcher shop. Mom bought THREE kinds of meat. The butcher gave Becky a slice of salami.

2

Go on

"Yum," said Becky.

Their fourth stop was the cheese store. Mom bought FOUR kinds of cheese. The cheese lady gave Becky a chunk of cheddar cheese.

"Thanks," said Becky.

Their fifth stop was the fruit stand. Mom bought FIVE different kinds of fruit. The fruit man gave Becky a purple plum.

"Yummy," said Becky.

Then they went home.

"Lunchtime," said Mom.

"LUNCH?" said Becky.

Go on

1 What were Becky and her mom doing?

Ⓐ going for a ride

Ⓑ baking cookies

Ⓒ shopping

2 How did Becky feel when people gave her things to eat.

Ⓐ happy

Ⓑ angry

Ⓒ sad

3 Why didn't Becky want any lunch?

Ⓐ She was sleepy.

Ⓑ She was full.

Ⓒ She wanted to play.

4

Go on

4 What did mom buy the most of?

All Smiles • Holistic Reading Assessment • Harcourt Brace School Publishers

Elephants Should Not Climb Trees

By Jeffie Ross Gordon
Illustrated by Jody Taylor

What happened to Elephant?

"I want to do something new," said Elephant. "I want to climb a tree."

Elephant shook a small tree with his trunk. "But not this tree," he said. "This tree is too small."

All Smiles • Holistic Reading Assessment • Harcourt Brace School Publishers

Bird flew down from a branch in the tree. "Elephants should not climb trees," she said.

But Elephant did not listen. He ambled away toward another tree.

Giraffe munched leaves from the bottom branches.

"And not this tree," said Elephant. "It is too tall.

Bird landed on Elephant's back. "Elephants should not climb trees," she said. But Elephant did not listen.

Soon Elephant came to a tree full of monkeys. "And not this tree, said Elephant. "It is too crowded."

Bird hopped up to Elephant's head. "Elephants should not climb trees," she said. But Elephant did not listen.

All Smiles • Holistic Reading Assessment • Harcourt Brace School Publishers

Elephant came to a thorn tree. A great hive of bees buzzed in the branches. "Not this tree," said Elephant. "It is too picky."

Bird landed on Elephant's trunk. "Elephants should not climb trees," she said. But Elephant did not listen.

Finally, Elephant came to the edge of the forest. He came to the last tree before the open plain. "This tree," he said. "This tree is just right!" Elephant began to climb.

Bird flew to Elephant's ear.

"ELEPHANTS SHOULD NOT CLIMB TREES!" she yelled.

Elephant still did not listen. Up, up, up he climbed. At last he sat on a branch. He could see all across the plain.

All Smiles • Holistic Reading Assessment • Harcourt Brace School Publishers

Bird soared to the top of the tree. She landed beside Elephant. "Elephants should not climb trees," she said.

"Why?" asked Elephant. "WHY should elephants not climb trees?"

"Because elephants cannot get down," said Bird. And she flew away.

Go on

5 What did Elephant want to do?

(A) go swimming

(B) climb a tree

(C) fly like a bird

6 The tree with the monkeys was too _____.

(A) crowded

(B) tall

(C) small

7 What does Bird keep telling Elephant?

(A) to stay away from bees

(B) not to climb trees

(C) not to eat leaves

Go on

8 What happened to Elephant at the end of the story?

 11

Just for Fun!

Think about the stories you just read. Then draw your favorite part of one of the stories. If you want, you may write to tell about your drawing.

All Smiles • Holistic Reading Assessment • Harcourt Brace School Publishers

13

Signatures

ALL SMILES

HOLISTIC READING ASSESSMENT

HARCOURT BRACE

ORLANDO ATLANTA AUSTIN BOSTON SAN FRANCISCO CHICAGO DALLAS NEW YORK
TORONTO LONDON

PART NO. 9997-17428-3

ISBN 0-15-308243-7 (PACKAGE OF 12)

1-5